52 GREAT
BRIDGE TIPS
ON DECLARER PLAY

52 GREAT
BRIDGE TIPS
ON DECLARER PLAY

David Bird

BATSFORD

First published in the United Kingdom in 2005 by
Batsford
151 Freston Road
London
W10 6TH

An imprint of Anova Books Company Ltd

EDITOR: Elena Jeronimidis

ISBN-13 9780713489774
ISBN-10 0 7134 8977 4

A CIP catalogue record for this book is available from the British Library.

10 9 8 7 6 5 4 3 2

Typeset in the United Kingdom by Ruth Edmondson
Printed and bound by Creative Print and Design, Ebbw Vale, Wales

This book can be ordered direct from the publisher at the website:
www.anovabooks.com, or try your local bookshop

Distributed in the United States and Canada by
Sterling Publishing Co.,
387 Park Avenue South, New York, NY 10016, USA

CONTENTS

CONTENTS continued

Tip 1

Disguise a singleton opening lead

A s declarer, you can sometimes be certain that the opening lead is a singleton. If your right-hand opponent holds the ace of the suit and can draw the same conclusion, he may defeat your contract by giving his partner a ruff.

In such a situation you must attempt to disguise the opening lead. You can often do this by hiding a lower spot-card in your hand. Suppose East opens 3◊ and West leads a diamond against your eventual game in a major suit. The diamond suit lies like this:

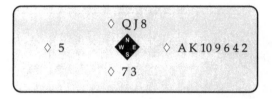

You play the queen from dummy and East wins with the king. Let's say first that you give the matter little thought and follow with the ◊3. Since West would not have led the ◊5 from ◊7-5, East will know for sure that his partner started with a singleton. Armed with this knowledge, it may suit him to cash the ◊A and play a third round of the suit.

To make life more difficult for East, you should follow with the ◊7 on the first trick. Since the ◊5 would be the normal lead from ◊5-3, East will now have no idea where the ◊3 is. It will be dangerous for him to cash the ◊A in case you have no more diamonds. You would then be able to ruff and score a trick with dummy's ◊J.

Your deceptive play will not always succeed, of course. East may be able to calculate: "We probably can't beat this contract unless declarer has a doubleton diamond." That's life. Sometimes defenders do the right thing. The point to remember is that you have absolutely nothing to lose by playing the ◊7! Much of the time East will be fooled and he'll let you make a contract that could have been defeated.

Let's see this style of play in the context of a full deal:

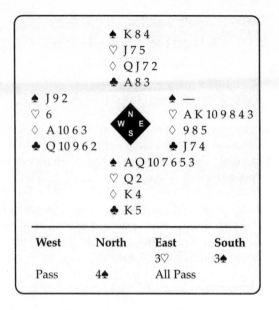

	♠ K 8 4		
	♡ J 7 5		
	◇ Q J 7 2		
	♣ A 8 3		

♠ J 9 2
♡ 6
◇ A 10 6 3
♣ Q 10 9 6 2

♠ —
♡ A K 10 9 8 4 3
◇ 9 8 5
♣ J 7 4

♠ A Q 10 7 6 5 3
♡ Q 2
◇ K 4
♣ K 5

West	North	East	South
		3♡	3♠
Pass	4♠	All Pass	

How would you play the spade game when West leads the ♡6 and East wins with the ♡K?

The normal play with this heart holding is to follow with the ♡2, assuring yourself of a heart trick. 'Normal' plays are not always right! Suppose you follow with the ♡2 here. Since West would not have led the ♡6 from ♡Q-6, East can be absolutely certain that the opening lead was a singleton. He will continue with the ♡A and then play a third round of hearts. This will promote a trump trick for West and you will go down whether you ruff high, ruff with the ♠10 or discard.

A better idea is to follow smoothly with the ♡Q at trick one. If East reads this card as a singleton, he will be reluctant to play the ♡A next. You might then be able to ruff and subsequently take a discard on the established ♡J in dummy (perhaps throwing a diamond if you held ◇A-x). He may decide to switch to a diamond instead, letting the contract through. There is not much point trying to analyse whether East should lead a diamond or his other top heart at trick two. The point is that he is certain to get it right unless you drop the ♡Q. Do this and you give East a problem. Sometimes he will go wrong.

On the next deal, you have to sacrifice a winner in a deceptive cause:

```
                    ♠ 5 3 2
                    ♡ 9 8 4 3
                    ◇ J 6 5
                    ♣ A Q 8
    ♠ 10 9 4                      ♠ 7 6
    ♡ A J 7 5          N          ♡ 10 2
    ◇ 7            W       E      ◇ A Q 10 9 8 4 2
    ♣ 10 7 6 5 4       S          ♣ 9 3
                    ♠ A K Q J 8
                    ♡ K Q 6
                    ◇ K 3
                    ♣ K J 2
```

West	North	East	South
		3◇	Dbl
Pass	3♡	Pass	3♠
Pass	4♠	All Pass	

3NT would have been more comfortable but you end in 4♠. How will you play this contract when West leads the ◇7 to East's ◇A?

The original declarer saw that the contract was doomed if he followed with the ◇3. East would give his partner a diamond ruff and in the fullness of time the defenders would surely score two heart tricks. He therefore dropped the ◇K under East's ace.

How do you think East reacted to this? He did exactly what you or I would have done with his cards. He switched to the ♡10! He was hoping that his partner held ♡A-Q-x-x and could score two heart tricks followed by a heart ruff. It didn't work out like that. Indeed, once East had failed to cash his ◇Q (or play a lower diamond) at trick two the contract could no longer be beaten. West won South's ♡K with the ♡A and switched to a club. (He knew from South's failure to raise hearts that East's ♡10 was not a singleton.) Declarer won the club switch, drew trumps and played queen and another heart to set up a discard for his losing diamond. Game made!

Sometimes West will lead a singleton in a side suit where you have four cards in dummy, facing four cards in your hand. Your task then will be to persuade East that it is you who hold the singleton. Look at this deal:

```
                    ♠ 5 3
                    ♡ A J 7 3
                    ◇ J 5 2
                    ♣ K J 7 3
  ♠ K J 9 7 4                          ♠ Q 10 6 2
  ♡ 6 4              N                  ♡ 10 2
  ◇ 10 8 6 4 3    W     E               ◇ K Q 9
  ♣ 2                S                  ♣ A 8 6 4
                    ♠ A 8
                    ♡ K Q 9 8 5
                    ◇ A 7
                    ♣ Q 10 9 5
```

West	North	East	South
			1♡
Pass	3♡	Pass	4♡
All Pass			

West leads the ♣2 against your heart game. How will you play?

It could hardly be clearer that the opening lead is a singleton. Clear to you, yes, but it may not be clear to East. Since a club ruff will leave you with four inescapable losers, you must try to persuade East that the opening lead is a fourth-best card from an honour holding. What is the best way to do this?

Whichever card you choose to play from the dummy, one thing you must not do is to follow with the ♣5 from your hand. East will then reason: "Partner would have led the ♣10 from ♣Q-10-9-2, so his ♣2 must be a singleton."

One possibility is to play the ♣J from dummy, giving the impression that you do not hold the queen or ten in your hand. You can then follow with the ♣9, painting a picture of ♣Q-10-5-2 with West. Alternatively you can play low from dummy and follow with the ♣9 or ♣10 from your hand. If East does place his partner with four clubs to the queen, he will be reluctant to lead back into dummy's ♣K-J-7, which might give you two discards.

So, don't give up when you fear that the opening lead is a singleton. By playing judiciously to the first trick, you may end up hearing that sweetest of sounds: "Why didn't you give me my ruff, partner?"

Tip 2

With one entry take the right finesse

It often happens that the high cards are located mainly in declarer's hand and dummy has only one entry. In this case you may have to judge which of two finesses you should take when you reach dummy for the first and last time. One good rule is to finesse in the suit where you will have a better residual chance in the other suit. Look at this typical deal:

```
                    ♠ 7 6 4
                    ♡ 10 8
                    ◇ J 6 3
                    ♣ A J 4 3 2
    ♠ Q 8                         ♠ 9 3 2
    ♡ Q 9 6 3 2       N           ♡ A J 7 5
    ◇ 9 4          W     E        ◇ K Q 10
    ♣ K Q 10 5        S           ♣ 9 7 6
                    ♠ A K J 10 5
                    ♡ K 4
                    ◇ A 8 7 5 2
                    ♣ 8
```

West	North	East	South
			1♠
Pass	2♣	Pass	4♠
All Pass			

West leads the ♣K against your game in spades. You win with dummy's ace and see that you are in dummy for the last time. Should you play a trump to the jack or a heart to the king?

There are two good reasons why you should play a heart. (Three if you include the fact that you have looked at the full diagram and can see that the ♡A is onside!) The first is that if a heart to the king wins, you will have gained a trick by the play. If you play a spade to the jack instead and this wins, you will not gain a trick when spades are 4-1 and East can still score his queen on the fourth round.

The second reason to play a heart is that if the ♡K loses to the ♡A with West, you will still have some residual chance of picking up the spades without loss. You will be able to play for the drop, succeeding when a defender holds a singleton or doubleton ♠Q.

Which finesse would you take on the next deal?

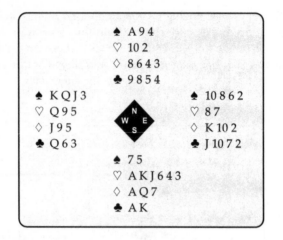

```
                    ♠ A 9 4
                    ♡ 10 2
                    ◊ 8 6 4 3
                    ♣ 9 8 5 4
  ♠ K Q J 3                        ♠ 10 8 6 2
  ♡ Q 9 5            N             ♡ 8 7
  ◊ J 9 5         W     E          ◊ K 10 2
  ♣ Q 6 3            S             ♣ J 10 7 2
                    ♠ 7 5
                    ♡ A K J 6 4 3
                    ◊ A Q 7
                    ♣ A K
```

West leads the ♠K against 4♡. You win the first (or second, it makes no difference) spade in dummy and see that you have a choice of red-suit finesses to take. What would your next play be?

The original declarer thought: "I can get the best of both worlds here. I will take the percentage line in trumps by leading the ♡2 to the ♡J. If the finesse loses to the ♡Q, dummy's ♡10 will become an entry and I can still take the diamond finesse!" This all came to pass and he made the contract, but do you think it was the best line?

Suppose instead that you take a similar line to that on the first deal. You finesse the ◊Q and then play for the drop in hearts. You will make the contract when the ◊K is onside (50%) or when it is offside but the ♡Q falls in two rounds (another 16.4%), giving a total of 66.4%.

How good was the original declarer's line? He would succeed when he could score six heart tricks with a successful finesse of the ♡J (36.8% for East holding ♡Q-x-x, ♡Q-x or a singleton ♡Q). He would succeed also if the heart finesse lost but a subsequent diamond finesse won. A skilful West would duck the ♡J when he held ♡Q-x-x-x, to kill the entry to dummy and prevent declarer from taking a diamond finesse. So this adds only another 18.4% – giving a relatively poor total of just 55.2%. A diamond finesse is easily best!

Here is a slightly more difficult deal where you again have a chance to return to dummy in the suit of the first finesse:

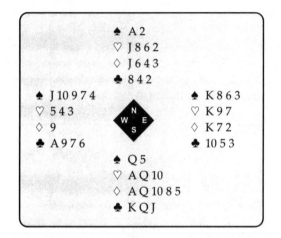

```
            ♠ A 2
            ♡ J 8 6 2
            ◇ J 6 4 3
            ♣ 8 4 2
♠ J 10 9 7 4              ♠ K 8 6 3
♡ 5 4 3         N         ♡ K 9 7
◇ 9          W     E      ◇ K 7 2
♣ A 9 7 6        S        ♣ 10 5 3
            ♠ Q 5
            ♡ A Q 10
            ◇ A Q 10 8 5
            ♣ K Q J
```

You reach 3NT and West leads the ♠J. It is a blow when East wins with the ♠K and clears the spade suit. How will you attempt to recover?

With so many spade winners out, you cannot afford to play on clubs. You will need to score eight tricks from the red suits without surrendering the lead. Let's suppose you lead a low diamond from dummy, finessing the queen. All will be well if East has a doubleton (or singleton) ◇K. Your ace will drop the king and you can return to dummy with the ◇J to finesse in hearts. When the cards lie as in the diagram you will go down, even though both the red kings are onside.

A better idea is to lead the ◇J from dummy, planning to unblock the ◇8 if East follows with a spot card. This will work just as well as a low card when East holds a singleton or doubleton ◇K. You will eventually return to dummy by leading the ◇5 to the ◇6. The benefit comes when the diamond suit lies as in the diagram. The ◇J will pin West's ◇9 and you will again be able to return to dummy with the ◇6 to lead the ♡J.

There are several possible reasons why it may not be good tactics to draw trumps straight away. One of them is that you need to use the entries provided by the trump suit in order to set up a side suit in dummy. Here is a straightforward example:

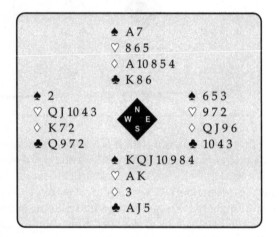

You venture a grand slam in spades after partner shows you two aces and one king. How will you play the contract when West leads the ♡Q?

There are two possible ways to dispose of the potential loser in clubs. You can finesse the ♣J or you can set up a long diamond for a discard. As usual, you do best to investigate the potential of a discard first, falling back on the finesse if necessary.

How does the play go? You win the heart lead in your hand, cross to the ◇A and ruff a diamond high. You then lead the ♠4 to dummy's ♠7 and ruff another diamond. You're in luck, for once, and the diamonds divide 4-3. You return to dummy with the ♠A and establish a long diamond by taking your third ruff in the suit. After drawing East's remaining trump, you return to dummy with the ♣K and take your well-earned discard on the long diamond. Grand slam made.

Does anything else strike you about that deal? If West had led a trump against the grand slam, as he was taught on his grandmother's knee, he would have defeated the slam. One of the necessary entries to dummy would have been removed prematurely.

On the next deal you must make the best use of entries in a side suit as well as those in the trump suit:

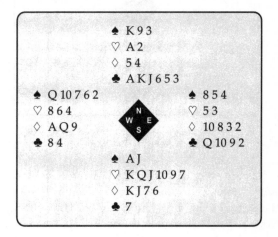

West leads the ♣6 against 6♡. You play low from dummy and East plays the ♠8. What is your plan?

You can score three spade tricks if you win with the first trick with the ♠J. What use is a third spade trick, though? Your general plan will be to set up and enjoy dummy's club suit and this will require several entries to dummy. You should therefore win the first trick with the ♣A, retaining the option to cross to the ♣K later. What next? Will you draw trumps?

Let's hope not because the ♡A may be needed as an entry to set up the clubs. At trick two you should cross to the ♣A. You ruff a club high, both defenders following, and continue with the king and ace of trumps. In case the clubs break 4-2 you ruff another club. You can then draw the outstanding trumps and cross to dummy by leading the ♠J to the ♠K. You discard three diamonds on the ♣K-J-6 and the contract is yours.

Sometimes dummy's trump suit will provide the required number of entries only if the defenders' trumps lie favourably. That's the case here:

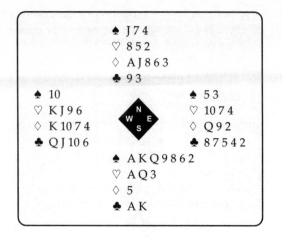

```
              ♠ J 7 4
              ♡ 8 5 2
              ◇ A J 8 6 3
              ♣ 9 3
♠ 10                        ♠ 5 3
♡ K J 9 6        N          ♡ 10 7 4
◇ K 10 7 4    W     E       ◇ Q 9 2
♣ Q J 10 6       S          ♣ 8 7 5 4 2
              ♠ A K Q 9 8 6 2
              ♡ A Q 3
              ◇ 5
              ♣ A K
```

How will you play 6♠ when West leads the ♣Q to your ace?

What prospects are there of avoiding a heart finesse by setting up the diamond suit? If only two trump entries to the dummy are available, you will need a defender to hold ◇K-Q or ◇K-Q-x. If three trump entries are available, you can establish a discard whenever the diamonds break 4-3.

You cross to the ◇A and ruff a diamond with the ♠8. Now, how can you conjure three trump entries to dummy? One possibility is to lead the ♠6 to the ♠7. When West started with ♠10-x, the ♠7 would give you one entry. You could subsequently lead the ♠9 to the ♠J and finally the ♠2 to the ♠4, achieving two further entries. There are two things wrong with this plan. If a finesse of the ♠7 fails, you will go down even when the ♡K is onside. Secondly, if West is a strong defender, he may insert the ♠10 from ♠10-x, killing one of the entries that you need.

A better idea is to lead the ♠9 to the ♠J. This allows you to benefit from the ♠10 being singleton, without giving the defenders any extra chance in exchange. When the ♠10 falls, as in the diagram, you will win with dummy's ♠J and ruff another diamond high. You then lead the ♠6 to dummy's ♠7 and ruff a fourth rounds of diamonds high, setting up a long card in the suit. Finally you overtake your ♠2 with the ♠4 and enjoy a heart discard on the thirteenth diamond. You seek an overtrick by finessing the ♡Q and are pleased to see the finesse fail. This means that your entry-creating play (leading the ♠9 on the first round of trumps) was necessary to make the slam.

If the lie of the cards prevented you from enjoying a discard on the diamonds, you would fall back on the heart finesse.

Tip 4

Use the fourth card in a suit for a throw-in

Suppose you hold a suit something like A-K-6-2 opposite Q-7-3. You play the top three cards, hoping for a 3-3 break but one of the defenders shows out on the third round. A time for despair? Not necessarily. You may be able to use the fourth card in the suit to execute a throw-in. Only one defender still has a card left in the suit, of course, so you can tell who your intended victim will be.

Let's see an example of the play:

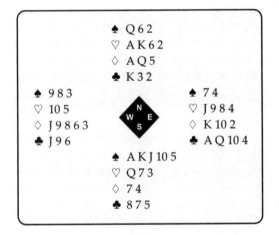

A contract of 3NT would have been better (particularly if played by North) but you arrive in 4♠. How will you play the contract when West leads the ♠3?

You win the trump lead and draw trumps in two further rounds. When you play the ♡Q, ♡A and ♡K, the suit fails to divide 3-3. No matter. Since it is East who holds the long heart, you can claim the contract! You lead the ♡6 to East's ♡J and discard a club loser from your hand. East must now return a club or a diamond, both of which will give you a tenth trick.

On some deals you may need to ruff the third round of a suit to prepare for a throw-in with the fourth card. That is what happens here:

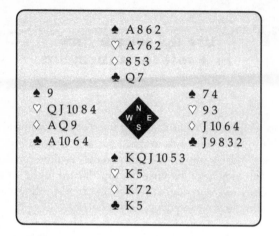

West, who opened the bidding with 1♡, leads the ♡Q against 4♠. How will you plan the play?

You should aim to eliminate clubs and throw West on lead with the fourth round of hearts. You win the heart lead with the king and draw trumps with the king and queen. You lead the ♣K to West's ♣A and win the club return in dummy. After cashing the ♡A, you ruff a heart in your hand and return to dummy with a trump. These cards remain:

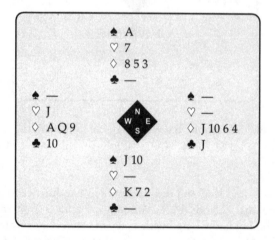

You lead the ♡7, throwing a diamond loser, and West has to give you a trick with his return. A diamond return will allow your ◊K to score. A club return will concede a ruff-and-discard.

Tip 5

Spurn a finesse to establish the suit

Taking a finesse is always tempting. (I used to think that the only 'planning the play' my mother ever did was to scan her hand and the dummy, looking for ace-queen combinations.) Sometimes, though, the entry position is such that you cannot afford to take a finesse in the suit that you are hoping to establish. Instead you must begin with the top card from the shorter holding. An example will make this clear:

```
                    ♠ A K 7 6 2
                    ♡ K 10
                    ◇ 10 6 5
                    ♣ Q 3 2
     ♠ Q 10                           ♠ J 8 5 4
     ♡ 8 2              N             ♡ A Q 5 4
     ◇ Q 8 7 3      W       E         ◇ K 9 2
     ♣ J 10 9 6 4       S             ♣ 8 5
                    ♠ 9 3
                    ♡ J 9 7 6 3
                    ◇ A J 4
                    ♣ A K 7
```

West	North	East	South
			1♡
Pass	1♠	Pass	1NT
Pass	3NT	All Pass	

West leads the ♣J against your no-trump game. You have six top tricks and the best chance of bumping up this to nine is to develop the heart suit. (This is better than setting up the spades. Even if spades break 3-3, this would give you only eight tricks and you would need an extra trick from one of the red suits.) How will you manage the play?

With unlimited entries to the South hand, you would broach the heart suit by playing a low card to dummy's ten. This would give you four heart tricks when West held ♡Q-x. To make 3NT, though, you need only three heart tricks. Let's see what might happen if you win the club lead in your hand and play a heart to the ten. East wins with the ♡Q and, if on form, will switch to the ◊K, attacking the entries to your hand. You win with the ◊A and play a second round of hearts to the ♡K. East holds up the ace and the contract can no longer be made. You have only one entry left to your hand (the ♣K) and the hearts are not yet established.

Many East players would not find the ◊K switch, it's true. However, there is no need to take any risks on the hand. You should win the club lead with the ♣Q and lead the ♡K from dummy. Since you still have three entries to the South hand, it will be an easy task to set up the heart suit and make the game.

Here is a similar example, this time in a suit contract. Again the distraction of a possible finesse would lead many players to go down.

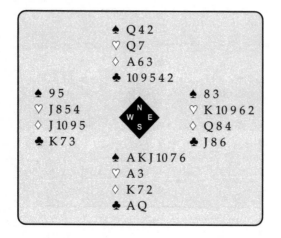

♠ Q 4 2
♡ Q 7
◊ A 6 3
♣ 10 9 5 4 2

♠ 9 5
♡ J 8 5 4
◊ J 10 9 5
♣ K 7 3

♠ 8 3
♡ K 10 9 6 2
◊ Q 8 4
♣ J 8 6

♠ A K J 10 7 6
♡ A 3
◊ K 7 2
♣ A Q

You reach a small slam in spades and West leads the ◊J, missing the deadly attack in hearts. How will you play the contract?

Suppose you win the diamond lead in dummy and finesse the ♣Q. Even if this finesse wins, you will not be in good shape. Two losers will remain in the red suits and, with only one entry left to the dummy and the long clubs there, you will have very little chance of disposing of them.

You need to set up the club suit and the best chance of doing this is to lead clubs from the South hand, preserving the two entries to dummy. You should win the diamond lead in your hand, with the king, and draw two rounds of trumps with the ace and king. It's not particularly critical but the suit happens to break 2-2. You continue with the ace and queen of clubs. If West wins with the ♣K and plays a second diamond, you will win with dummy's ◇A. When you lead the ♣10, the appearance of East's ♣J will spare you a guess in the suit. You will ruff in the South hand and return to dummy with the ♠Q to enjoy two discards on the established clubs.

Holding up the ♣K would do West no good at all. You would cross to the ♠Q, establish the clubs with a ruff and return to the ◇A to throw two losers and claim an overtrick. Playing in this fashion, you make the contract whenever clubs break 3-3 or the ♣J falls doubleton.

Tip
6

Discard losers to
avoid an overruff

hen you and your left-hand opponent both hold length in the same suit, there may be danger that your right-hand opponent can overruff the dummy. You can sometimes rescue the situation by discarding the losers in your hand. Here is a fairly obvious example of the technique:

```
                    ♠ 9 6 4 3
                    ♡ 6 3
                    ◊ A J 10 4
                    ♣ Q 10 6
      ♠ A 2                          ♠ 10 8
      ♡ K Q J 10 5 2      N          ♡ 8 4
      ◊ K 8 3          W     E       ◊ 9 7 5 2
      ♣ 8 5               S          ♣ A 9 7 4 2
                    ♠ K Q J 7 5
                    ♡ A 9 7
                    ◊ Q 6
                    ♣ K J 3
```

West	North	East	South
1♡	Pass	Pass	1♠
Pass	2♣	Pass	4♠
All Pass			

West leads the ♡K against your spade game and East follows with the ♡8. How will you play the contract?

Suppose you win with the ace and lead a trump honour. West will win immediately, cash a heart winner and lead a third round of hearts. East can overruff dummy's ♠9 with the ♠10 and that will be one down.

To avoid this unseemly fate, you must aim to discard your third heart before you play trumps. At trick two you lead the ◊Q. Whether or not West elects to cover, you will score three diamond tricks and can throw one of your heart losers. When you play a trump to the king and ace,

---

52 Great Bridge Tips on Declarer Play

West cannot beat the contract. He can cash one heart winner but a third round of hearts would be unproductive. Since you have no hearts left in the South hand, East cannot enjoy a successful overruff.

On the next deal the recommended technique (discarding losers at an early stage) will offer you two chances of success:

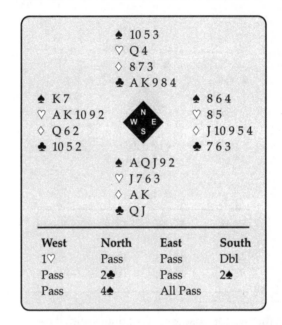

	♠ 10 5 3	
	♡ Q 4	
	◊ 8 7 3	
	♣ A K 9 8 4	
♠ K 7		♠ 8 6 4
♡ A K 10 9 2		♡ 8 5
◊ Q 6 2		◊ J 10 9 5 4
♣ 10 5 2		♣ 7 6 3
	♠ A Q J 9 2	
	♡ J 7 6 3	
	◊ A K	
	♣ Q J	

West	North	East	South
1♡	Pass	Pass	Dbl
Pass	2♣	Pass	2♠
Pass	4♠	All Pass	

West plays the two top heart honours and East confirms the expected 5-2 break by playing high-low. How will you play when West continues with the ♡10?

Only 13 points are out so you can be virtually certain that West holds the ♠K. At trick three you ruff high, with dummy's ♠10, and East discards a club. What now?

After East's discard there are only five clubs out. Since one or other defender is bound to ruff at some stage, it may seem that it cannot help you to play three rounds of clubs, aiming to discard your last heart. This is not the case. You should cash the ace of trumps next. If the king of trumps happens to fall, you will simply draw trumps. When the cards lie as in the diagram, both defenders will follow with a low trump. Now you play the ♣Q, ♣A and ♣K. When East ruffs, as he must, you overruff and play the queen of trumps. There are now no more trumps out and you make the game.

What was the second possibility that I mentioned? Suppose you embark on this line and West has a doubleton club. You would discard your ♡J on the third club and West would have to ruff with the ♠K. Again you would lose only three tricks – two in hearts and one to the king of trumps. Here is a more complicated example of this style of play:

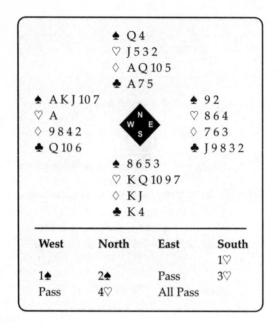

	♠ Q 4	
	♡ J 5 3 2	
	◊ A Q 10 5	
	♣ A 7 5	

♠ A K J 10 7		♠ 9 2
♡ A		♡ 8 6 4
◊ 9 8 4 2		◊ 7 6 3
♣ Q 10 6		♣ J 9 8 3 2

	♠ 8 6 5 3	
	♡ K Q 10 9 7	
	◊ K J	
	♣ K 4	

West	North	East	South
			1♡
1♠	2♣	Pass	3♡
Pass	4♡	All Pass	

West cashes the two top spades and continues with the ♠J. How will you tackle the contract?

If you ruff low, it is obvious what will happen. East will overruff and you will still have the ♡A to lose. That will be one down. So, you ruff with dummy's jack of trumps and East discards a diamond. What now?

If you play a trump West will win with the ace and lead another spade, allowing East to overruff the dummy. Instead you must put East under pressure by playing diamonds. You play the ◊K, overtake the ◊J with the ◊A and play the ◊Q. East, who threw a diamond at trick three, is now out of the suit. If he fails to ruff, you will throw your last spade and make the contract easily. East ruffs, therefore, and you overruff.

You return to dummy with the ♣A and lead the ◊10. Once again East has to ruff. You overruff and lead the king of trumps. West wins with the ace and East follows with his last trump. The contract is yours. In the fullness of time you will be able to ruff your last spade.

Determining the best play within a single suit is far from easy and, even in a world championship, you will often see players choosing different lines. Hardly anyone calculates using actual percentages. The best idea is to consider the various likely lines of play and to see which one catches the most combinations. In the present Tip we will look at some situations where you can pick up a doubleton honour that is held by one of the defenders. This situation is doubtless familiar to you:

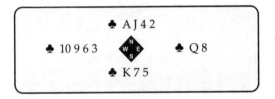

If you need all four club tricks, you must finesse the ♣J and hope that West holds ♣Q-x-x. Suppose instead that three club tricks will give you the contract. It is then better to cash the ace and king first, leading towards the jack on the third round. You still make the three tricks you need when West holds the ♣Q or clubs break 3-3. The benefit of the safety play is that you also score three tricks when East has ♣Q-x.

With many such single-suit plays, you can find an echo of the position if you move all the honours down one notch. Let's try it here:

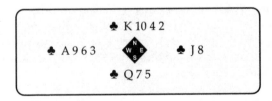

Yes, it works! If you need a full three tricks from the suit, you will play a club to the queen and, whether or not this card wins, subsequently finesse the ♣10. You will succeed in your objective when West holds ♣J-x-x or ♣A-J-x, also when East holds a singleton ♣A or a doubleton ♣A-J.

Now suppose that you need only two club tricks for the contract. Again you begin with a club to the queen and ace. On the next round you cash the king, picking up the case of a doubleton jack with East. If the ♣J does not fall on the second round, you will lead towards dummy's ♣10 on the third round.

Try the next deal, which features a less well-known combination:

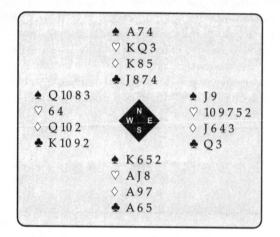

```
              ♠ A 7 4
              ♡ K Q 3
              ◇ K 8 5
              ♣ J 8 7 4
  ♠ Q 10 8 3              ♠ J 9
  ♡ 6 4        N          ♡ 10 9 7 5 2
  ◇ Q 10 2  W   E         ◇ J 6 4 3
  ♣ K 10 9 2    S         ♣ Q 3
              ♠ K 6 5 2
              ♡ A J 8
              ◇ A 9 7
              ♣ A 6 5
```

West leads the ♠3 against 3NT and you win East's ♠J with the ♠K. There is no point in a hold-up because West's fourth-best ♠3 tells you that he has only a four-card suit. Apart from that, a switch to diamonds might prove unwelcome. How will you continue?

You have eight top tricks and the only solid chance of a ninth trick lies in the club suit. What is the best way to play that suit, though?

You can easily establish an extra club trick when the suit breaks 3-3, so you must aim to pick up some of the 4-2 breaks. If either defender holds ♣K-Q doubleton, you will score an extra trick with dummy's ♣J. What if West holds something like ♣Q-9? That's no good because East would then hold K-10-3-2, sitting over dummy's ♣J. You would lose tricks to the ♣Q and to both of East's honours.

What if East has a doubleton club honour, as in the diagram? You can pick this up by cashing the ♣A and ducking the second round of the suit. East's honour will appear on the second round and you can lead towards dummy's ♣J on the third round. Playing in this way, you will still make two club tricks when the suit breaks 3-3. You give yourself the extra chance that East holds ♣Q-x or ♣K-x.

For a moment let's switch horses and look at this combination from the point of view of the defender in the West seat. Suppose you are West, defending a no-trump contract, and the club suit looks like this:

When a competent declarer plays ace and another club, you should not rush in with one of your honours. Play low smoothly! If declarer knows what he is doing, he will play low in the dummy and your partner will score his ♣10.

(If declarer held a doubleton ♣A, you might do better in the West seat by rising with an honour in the second position. However, it is most unlikely that he would choose to play on such a flimsy suit.)

Now resume the declarer's seat. Since ducking in dummy on the second round wins against ♣K-x or ♣Q-x with East and rising with dummy's ♣J wins against ♣10-x or ♣9-x, you may perhaps think there is nothing much between the two lines. Of course there is! The point is that few of the world's defenders are good enough to play low when they hold ♣K-Q-x-x in the second seat. When West does play low from four cards, the odds are therefore hugely stacked in favour of East's remaining card being the king or queen.

Try one more contract on the same theme:

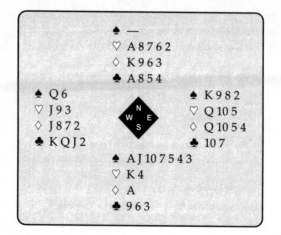

West leads the ♣K against 4♠. You win with dummy's ♣A and cross to the ◊A. After drawing one round of trumps with the ace, you return to dummy with the ♡A to discard one of your club losers on the ◊K.

So far, so good. You return to your hand with the ♡K and must now restrict your trump losers to two. This is the position in the trump suit:

Many players would lead the ♠J next but it is not the right play. As you see, playing in this way will cost you the contract. You will lose three trump tricks and one club.

If the trumps started out 3-3, you are safe whether you lead the jack or a low card on the second round (unless the defenders can arrange a trump promotion). To give yourself a chance when the trumps were divided 4-2 originally, you should lead a low card on the second round. Here West will win with the bare ♠Q. When you regain the lead you will use your ♠J-10 to restrict East to one further trick from his ♠K-9.

Tip 8   Take the defender by surprise

Suppose you reach a contract such as 6♡ and win the opening lead. The defenders will no doubt expect you to draw trumps next. If instead you flash out a card in a side suit, the defender in the second seat may be taken by surprise. He may either make a mistake or give you some key information.

There is nothing in the least bit unethical in such a tactic by declarer. You are entitled to apply pressure on the defenders by timing the play as you wish. For example, there is a right and a wrong way to play this contract:

```
              ♠ Q 10 3
              ♡ K 8 6 2
              ◇ K 2
              ♣ K J 9 2
♠ 9 7 6 2              ♠ J 8 4
♡ 4           N         ♡ 9 7
◇ J 10 9 4   W   E     ◇ 8 7 6 5 3
♣ A 10 7 6     S       ♣ Q 8 4
              ♠ A K 5
              ♡ A Q J 10 5 3
              ◇ A Q
              ♣ 5 3
```

West	North	East	South
	1♣	Pass	1♡
Pass	2♡	Pass	6♡
All Pass			

West leads the ◇J against your small slam in hearts. Suppose you draw trumps and play your winners in spades and diamonds, hoping to get some information about the defenders' hands. When you eventually lead a club towards dummy, it will be totally obvious to West that the defenders need two club tricks to beat the contract. He will play low smoothly and you will be faced with a very awkward guess.

You can give yourself a much better chance by winning with the ◇A and immediately playing a club. West may not be expecting this. Even if he is alert, he will have a difficult decision to make. Perhaps you have a singleton club, and a possible loser in some other suit. In that case you might well choose to play clubs early, before the loser elsewhere has become apparent. West is much more likely to rise with the ♣A if you play a club at trick two than if you delay the 'moment of truth' until later. He may also give the game away by thinking momentarily whether to rise with the ace, before playing low. (If he paused noticeably when holding the ♣Q and not the ♣A, this would be unethical play and you would be entitled to redress.)

Perhaps you think that the defenders you face are cool customers and will produce a smooth low club every time. You may be right, but if West does play low he may find that the full deal looks like this:

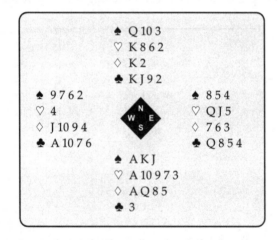

Again you bid to 6♡, win the opening ◇J lead with the ◇A and immediately play the ♣3. If West plays low, you will rise with the king (a discard on the clubs is no use to you and your sole objective here is to avoid a club loser). The king will win and you can subsequently afford a loser in the trump suit.

There is no way that West can distinguish between these two layouts. Provided you play a club at trick two rather than later, when the position has become clear, West will be put to a difficult guess and will often go wrong.

Let's look at a different situation where a defender is likely to assist you when put to the test early in the play:

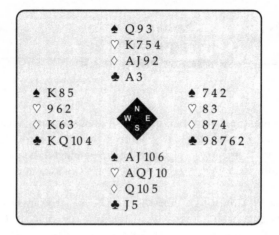

♠ Q 9 3
♡ K 7 5 4
◇ A J 9 2
♣ A 3

♠ K 8 5
♡ 9 6 2
◇ K 6 3
♣ K Q 10 4

♠ 7 4 2
♡ 8 3
◇ 8 7 4
♣ 9 8 7 6 2

♠ A J 10 6
♡ A Q J 10
◇ Q 10 5
♣ J 5

Spurred on by your two recent successes in 6♡, you decide to bid the same contract one more time. How will you play the slam when West leads the ♣K?

You win the opening lead with dummy's ♣A and let's suppose first that you draw trumps in three rounds. What now? If you can take a successful finesse in either spades or diamonds, you will be able to throw a club loser on the fourth round of that suit. Should your chosen finesse fail, the defenders will quickly cash a club trick and you will be one down even if the other finesse would have proved successful. It looks as if you will have to guess which finesse to take.

Against most of the world's defenders you can make the slam when either of the kings is onside! You should win the opening lead with dummy's ♣A and immediately play the ♠Q. If East holds the ♠K he may be caught by surprise. He will no doubt have expected you to draw trumps first and may have made no general plan about defending the contract as a whole. You can be sure that most of the world's defenders will cover in the East seat if they hold the ♠K. This will end your problems. With trumps breaking 3-2, you will be able to draw trumps and play three more rounds of spades to dispose of dummy's club loser. A club ruff in dummy will then give you the contract.

What if the cards lie as in the diagram and East does not cover the ♠Q? It will then be a reasonable assumption that West holds the ♠K. You will win the first round of spades with the ace, draw trumps and rely on a successful diamond finesse instead. Playing in this fashion, you will have a great chance of success when either the ♠K or the ◇K is onside. Roll up, roll up, two chances for the price of one!

Tip

9

Choose the line requiring the least good luck

Few players use actual percentages when they are calculating the best line in a contract. Beginners learn at an early stage that a finesse is a 50% prospect. After they have played the game a while, they may also hear that a 2-2 break is a 40% chance and a 3-3 break around 36%. Anything much beyond that is left to the Mathematical Tables section of the *Bridge Encyclopedia*. Even if the mere thought of percentages gives you a headache, there are a few basic rules that you can use when comparing two lines of play. We will see some of these as we work out the best line of play on a few deals. Try this grand slam first:

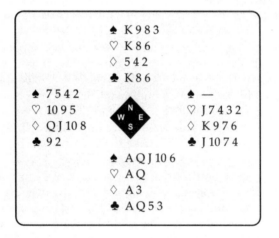

One of your better auctions carries you to 7♠ and West leads the ◊Q. You win with the ace and play a round of trumps, East discarding a heart. How can you recover from this setback?

One possible plan is to draw trumps straight away. You can then cash the ♡A and ♡Q, and cross to dummy with the ♣K to throw your diamond loser on the ♡K. You will make the contract when clubs break 3-3.

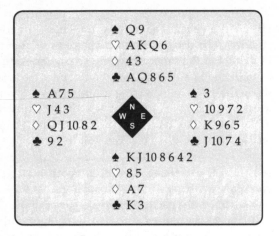

```
                    ♠ Q 9
                    ♡ A K Q 6
                    ◊ 4 3
                    ♣ A Q 8 6 5
    ♠ A 7 5                          ♠ 3
    ♡ J 4 3           N              ♡ 10 9 7 2
    ◊ Q J 10 8 2   W     E           ◊ K 9 6 5
    ♣ 9 2             S              ♣ J 10 7 4
                    ♠ K J 10 8 6 4 2
                    ♡ 8 5
                    ◊ A 7
                    ♣ K 3
```

West leads the ◊Q against 6♠. How will you play the contract?

You must dispose of the diamond loser before turning to the trump suit. Should you rely on hearts or clubs to provide the discard?

There are seven hearts out and only six clubs. When you have an even number of cards missing (four, six or eight) an even break is always against the odds. When you have an odd number of cards out, the most even division possible (a 4-3 break of seven cards, for example) is always with the odds. So, it is more likely that both defenders will follow to three rounds of hearts than to three rounds of clubs. When you play on hearts the defenders do indeed follow all the way. You discard your diamond loser and then draw trumps, making the contract easily.

There are two other points to make before we move to the next deal. The first is that you may survive if East holds only a doubleton in the side suit that you play first. Suppose East started with a doubleton heart. If he ruffs the ♡Q with a low trump, you can overruff and turn to the club suit. You will still get your diamond away if clubs are 3-3, or if the defender with a doubleton club has only the ♠A available for ruffing.

The second point concerns the defence. Suppose you play the deal in the recommended fashion, winning the opening lead and playing the ♡A and ♡K. West should drop the ♡J on the second round to make it look as if he started with only two hearts. If you fall for this deception and try your luck in clubs instead you will go down.

We will end with a deal where you have to compare the chance of a finesse with that of a favourable break in a different suit:

On some deals you can improve your chances by playing on the 4-3 sui (clubs, here) before drawing all the trumps. You know already that Wes has the long trumps. If he also holds four clubs, you can play the ♣K, ♣A and ♣Q and ruff the fourth round in dummy. On the present deal such a plan is most unlikely to succeed. You would need to discard your diamond loser on the ♡K before drawing trumps, so West would have to hold three hearts in addition to four trumps and four clubs. This would leave him with only two diamonds, making his ◊Q lead a most unlikely choice against a grand slam. What else can you try?

A better idea is to ruff two diamonds in the South hand, playing the contract as a dummy reversal. How does the play go? At trick three, after you have found out about the bad trump break, you cash the ♡A and ♡Q. You then cross to the ♣K and throw your remaining diamond on the ♡K. You ruff a diamond with the ♠10 in your hand and return to dummy with the ♠6 to the ♠9. You then ruff dummy's last diamond with the ♠J and return to dummy by overtaking the ♠Q with the ♠K. Finally you draw West's last trump and claim the contract.

Is this a better line than simply drawing trumps and hoping for the clubs to break 3-3? It sure is. All you need is for West to follow to three rounds of hearts, allowing you to discard your diamond loser. Since there are eight hearts out, and only six clubs, West is much more likely to hold three or more cards in hearts than in clubs.

Here is a simpler deal that illustrates the same theme:

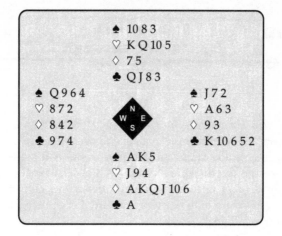

West leads the ◊2 against 6◊. How will you play the slam?

You have two potential losers in the South hand, a heart and a spade. You would like to discard your spade loser on the fourth round of hearts, but competent defenders will prevent this by holding up the ♡A until the third round. (West will give a count signal of the ♡2 on the first round, telling East that he has an odd number of cards in the suit.) So, you will be able to discard the spade only when the ♡A is singleton or doubleton, preventing a hold-up. What other chance is there?

The other possibility is a ruffing finesse in clubs. You win the trump lead, draw trumps and cash the ♣A. When you play a heart to the ten, East has to hold up or you will enjoy three heart tricks. Taking advantage of being in the dummy, you lead the ♣Q. If East covers with the ♣K, you will ruff and return to dummy in hearts to throw your spade loser on the established ♣J. If instead East plays low on the ♣Q, you will discard the spade loser immediately.

How do you compare the two lines of play? The ruffing finesse in clubs is a 50% prospect. What is the chance of the ♡A falling in two rounds? The chance of a 4-2 heart break is 48%, but the ♡A will lie with the doubleton only one third of the time, which is 16%. Not close, is it? You should take the ruffing finesse.

**Steal a trick
by leading through
a high card**

Imagine you are playing in 3NT with only one stopper left in the opponents' main suit. Unfortunately you need to set up extra tricks in two different suits. How can you give yourself the best chance of doing this before the defenders can enjoy the long cards in their own suit? The answer may be to lead through a defender's high card, making it very expensive for him to rise with the card. Let's see this technique in the context of a full deal:

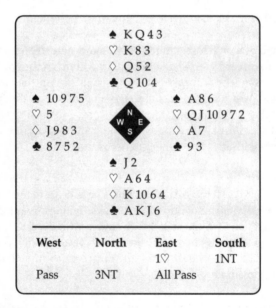

	♠ K Q 4 3	
	♡ K 8 3	
	◊ Q 5 2	
	♣ Q 10 4	
♠ 10 9 7 5		♠ A 8 6
♡ 5		♡ Q J 10 9 7 2
◊ J 9 8 3		◊ A 7
♣ 8 7 5 2		♣ 9 3
	♠ J 2	
	♡ A 6 4	
	◊ K 10 6 4	
	♣ A K J 6	

West	North	East	South
		1♡	1NT
Pass	3NT	All Pass	

West, who knows his duty when partner has bid a suit, leads the ♡5 against your contract of 3NT. What is your plan?

You have six top tricks in clubs and hearts, and must develop three more tricks from spades and diamonds. What will happen if you win the opening heart lead with the ace and lead the ♠J? East will take his ace immediately and clear the heart suit. Two extra spade tricks have brought your total to eight but you will not score any tricks from the diamond suit. The moment that you play a diamond, East will fly in with the ◊A and cash enough hearts to beat the contract.

Suppose instead that you win the lead with dummy's ♡K and lead a low diamond. That's no good either. East can rise with the ◊A and clear the hearts; since the diamond suit is not good, you will go one down.

To make the contract, you must win with dummy's ♡K and lead a low spade towards your hand. If East rises with the ♠A, you will have three spade tricks – enough for the contract. If instead East plays low, you will win with the ♠J, return to dummy with the ♣10 and lead a diamond towards your hand. If East rises with the ◊A, you will have two diamond tricks for the contract. If he ducks, you will win with the ◊K and set up your ninth trick in spades. Now try this one:

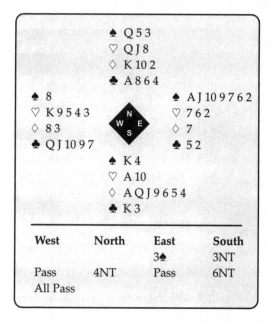

	♠ Q 5 3	
	♡ Q J 8	
	◊ K 10 2	
	♣ A 8 6 4	

♠ 8		♠ A J 10 9 7 6 2
♡ K 9 5 4 3		♡ 7 6 2
◊ 8 3		◊ 7
♣ Q J 10 9 7		♣ 5 2

	♠ K 4	
	♡ A 10	
	◊ A Q J 9 6 5 4	
	♣ K 3	

West	North	East	South
		3♠	3NT
Pass	4NT	Pass	6NT
All Pass			

How will you play 6NT when West leads the ♣Q?

You have ten tricks on top and must look to the major suits to establish two further tricks. Suppose you win the club lead in dummy and play a heart to the ten. When the finesse fails you will go down, losing one heart and one spade. A better idea, after winning the first trick with the ♣A, is to lead a low spade through East's ace. If East rises with the ace, you will score the two extra tricks you need with your spade honours. If instead East plays low, you will have one extra trick in the bag and you will have exhausted West's spade holding. You can return to dummy with a diamond and finesse hearts into what has become the safe hand. The finesse loses, as it happens, but you now have twelve tricks.

Tip

11

Tempt a cover to save a queen guess

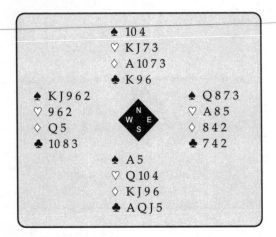

The defenders' adage 'always cover an honour with an honour' is wrong more often than it is right. The good news for you, as declarer, is that there are thousands of defenders out there who regard covering an honour as a sacred duty. Take advantage of it! Deals such as the following are commonplace:

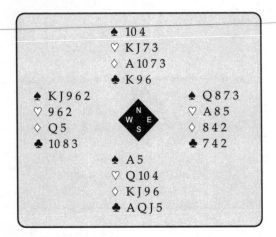

```
                    ♠ 10 4
                    ♡ K J 7 3
                    ◇ A 10 7 3
                    ♣ K 9 6
    ♠ K J 9 6 2              ♠ Q 8 7 3
    ♡ 9 6 2          N       ♡ A 8 5
    ◇ Q 5         W     E    ◇ 8 4 2
    ♣ 10 8 3         S       ♣ 7 4 2
                    ♠ A 5
                    ♡ Q 10 4
                    ◇ K J 9 6
                    ♣ A Q J 5
```

West leads the ♣6 against 3NT and you see that you have seven top tricks. How will you plan the play?

You can throw your heart suit out of the nearest window, since the defenders will have at least four spade tricks to go with their ♡A. To make the contract, you will need to score four diamond tricks. How should you play the suit?

With eight diamonds between the hands, the odds favour finessing against the queen rather than playing for the drop. Which defender is more likely to hold the ◇Q, though? The correct answer is: "I have no idea!" If you were forced to guess, you might as well toss a coin.

Against defenders of an average standard, you can set a small trap. Suppose you win the second spade and lead the ◇J from your hand. If West is a member of the 'always cover' brigade, he will play the ◇Q when he holds it. You will then have the four diamond tricks that you need. If instead West follows with a low diamond, you will overtake with dummy's ◊A and finesse East for the queen by leading the ◊10 and running it.

By playing in this fashion you will make the contract (against moderate opposition, who always cover) whichever defender holds the missing queen! Of course, it is a mistake for West to cover the ◊J. Those who do cover may perhaps think that this is the situation:

◊ A 10 7 3

◊ Q 5   ◊ K 9 4

◊ J 8 6 2

Now it would gain a trick for the defence if West covered the ◊J, thereby promoting East's ◊K-9 into two tricks. Do you see the flaw in this argument? With such a diamond holding South would not lead the jack on the first round! He would of course lead low to the ◊10, scoring three diamond tricks when West holds a doubleton honour, as well as when he has both honours. As a defender, it is usually best to assume that declarer will not lead an honour unless he can afford (and would welcome) the honour to be covered.

Note that you can afford to employ this queen-finding trap only when you hold sufficient spot cards to guard against a 4-1 break in the suit. The original declarer came to grief on this deal:

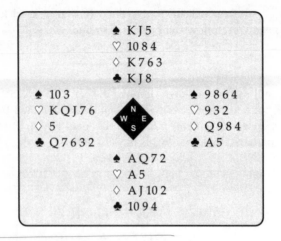

West led the ♡K against 3NT and declarer won the second round of the suit. Seeing that he needed four diamond tricks, he assumed his most innocent expression and led the ◊J from his hand at trick three. When West played low, declarer placed the ◊Q with East and rose with dummy's ◊K. A subsequent finesse of declarer's ◊10 brought good news and bad news. The finesse succeeded all right but West showed out and the contract could no longer be made.

Against defenders of a reasonable standard, those who are not likely to cover an honour automatically, declarer's play was against the odds. With this particular diamond holding he could pick up ◊Q-x-x-x with East but not with West. He should therefore have played East for the missing queen.

To pick up ◊Q-x-x-x with East, declarer could not afford to waste his ◊J on a fishing expedition. He should simply have played the ◊2 to the king and finessed the ◊10 on the way back. With his ◊A-J intact, he could then have returned to dummy with a spade and taken a second diamond finesse. That would give him four diamond tricks and the contract.

Tip 12

Use elimination play to survive a 4-1 break

The basic idea of elimination play is no doubt familiar to you. Playing in a suit contract, you draw trumps and eliminate one or two of the side suits. You then throw a defender on lead, forcing him to give you a trick in some way. In this Tip we will explore how you can use elimination play to protect yourself against a possible 4-1 break in a side suit. Look at this deal, for example:

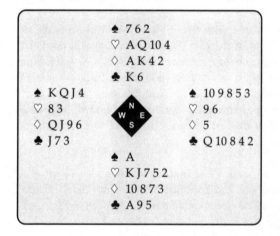

You open 1♡ on the South cards and arrive in 6♡ against silent opposition. How will you play the slam when West leads the ♠K?

You win with the ♠A and draw trumps in two rounds. If diamonds break 3-2 there will be no problem. In case the suit breaks 4-1, you should set up an elimination position. You cross to the ♣K and ruff a spade. You then cash the ♣A, ruff a club and ruff dummy's last spade. Both the black suits have now been eliminated and the defenders will not be able to lead a black suit without giving you a ruff-and-discard. The lead is in the South hand and these cards remain:

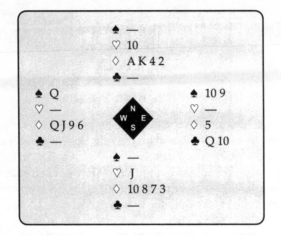

If West had started with ♠K-Q-J-x-x he would probably have overcalled at the one level. It therefore seems that East still holds two spades and cannot therefore hold four diamonds. If anyone holds four diamonds, it will be West. What can you do about it? The answer is to lead the ◊7 from your hand and run the card if West follows with the ◊6 or the ◊5. If East wins with a singleton queen, jack or nine, he will have to give you a ruff-and-discard. If instead he has a diamond to return, the suit will surely break 3-2.

What will happen if West chooses to cover the ◊7 with the ◊9? You will win with the ace and continue with a low diamond to your ten. East shows out and West wins with one of his diamond honours. He will then have to give you a ruff-and-discard or lead away from his other honour, allowing you to run the card. The slam is yours.

Now suppose that you had exactly the same North and South cards but West had made an overcall in spades. The odds would then tilt and East would become the favourite (if anyone) to hold four diamonds. How would you play the slam then?

Assuming you were again blessed with a 2-2 trump break, you would draw trumps and eliminate the black suits as before. When West follows to three rounds of clubs, his shape may be 6-2-1-4. You would then cash the ◊A, gaining immediately if West's singleton happened to be the queen or the jack. On the second round you would lead a low diamond towards your ten. If East still had ◊Q-J-x remaining, he would have to win with one honour and lead away from the other honour (or give you a ruff-and-discard).

There are many other 4-4 holdings where setting up an elimination position will allow you to survive a 4-1 break. Look at this one:

With trumps in both hands and the other two side suits eliminated, you lead low towards dummy and insert the ◊9 if West follows with the ◊4 or ◊5. East wins the trick and is endplayed. If he returns one of his two remaining honours, you will win with the ace and take the marked finesse on the third round. If instead East won the first round with a singleton diamond honour, he would have to give you a ruff-and-discard.

What would happen if West had played an honour on the first round of diamonds? You could then score the three tricks you need either by ducking (and running an honour continuation to the king) or by winning with the ace and playing a second round to the 8. Now try this:

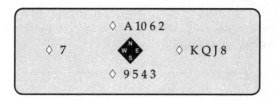

You set up an elimination position and play low to the ◊10 (or low to the ◊9). You will score two diamond tricks however the suit lies. Finally, assume you have no honours at all in your main side suit:

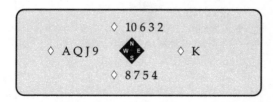

Here, aiming for one trick from the suit, you simply duck the first round. Unless a defender holds ◊A-K-Q-J, you will achieve your goal.

Tip	Choose between	
13	**a finesse and a**	
	ruffing finesse	

S uppose you are playing in a suit contract and hold a side suit something like this:

```
        ♣ A Q J 3
           N
        W     E
           S
        ♣ 7
```

Should you take a normal finesse in the suit, leading low to dummy's queen? Or would it be better to cross to the ♣A and lead the ♣Q from dummy, planning to ruff in your hand if East covers with the ♣K? How should you choose between these alternatives?

It may seem at first glance that it is merely a guess as to which defender will hold the missing king. Usually this is not the main consideration. Look at this deal, for example:

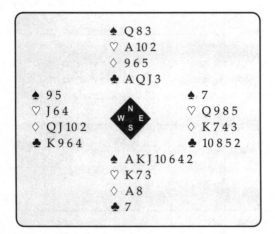

```
                ♠ Q 8 3
                ♡ A 10 2
                ◇ 9 6 5
                ♣ A Q J 3
  ♠ 9 5                          ♠ 7
  ♡ J 6 4          N             ♡ Q 9 8 5
  ◇ Q J 10 2    W     E          ◇ K 7 4 3
  ♣ K 9 6 4        S             ♣ 10 8 5 2
                ♠ A K J 10 6 4 2
                ♡ K 7 3
                ◇ A 8
                ♣ 7
```

West leads the ◇Q against 6♠ and you see that you have two potential losers in the red suits. After drawing trumps, will you take a normal finesse in clubs (leading the ♣7 to the ♣Q) or will you cross to the ♣A and take a ruffing finesse (running the ♣Q)?

Was your answer: "West has the ♣K, anyone can see that, so I'm going to take a normal finesse of the ♣Q and discard the diamond loser on the ♣A."? No cigar, if so. Lead a low club to the queen and you will go down if the finesse fails. East will score the ♣K and a diamond trick. Take a ruffing finesse instead and the contract is guaranteed. You cross to the ♣A and lead the ♣Q, discarding your diamond loser. No matter if the ruffing finesse loses to West's ♣K. Dummy's ♣J will be good for a discard of your heart loser and you will still make the slam.

The next deal illustrates the same principle, even though the two possible finesses are in different suits.

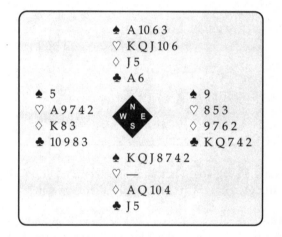

How will you play 6♠ when West leads the ♣10?

When the deal first arose, declarer said to himself: "I will have to take the diamond finesse anyway. If it succeeds, I can throw a club loser from dummy and make an overtrick." He won the club lead with dummy's ace, drew trumps and ran the ◊J. West won with the ◊K and played another club, putting the slam one down.

It was a poor effort by declarer. The diamond finesse gave him a 50% chance of making the slam, yes, but the ruffing heart finesse would have given him a 100% chance. After drawing trumps, he should have led the ♡K, discarding the last club from the South hand. The ruffing finesse would lose, as it happens, but dummy's ♡Q-J-10 would then be good for three diamond discards.

Playing on hearts instead of diamonds would be the right play even if dummy's hearts were just ♡K-Q-5-3-2. You lead the ♡K and ruff if East produces the ♡A, later crossing to dummy to discard your club loser on the ♡Q. If instead East does not produce the ♡A, you will discard a club. If the 50% ruffing finesse fails, you are not necessarily dead. You can still fall back on the diamond finesse! Two chances are better than one.

We will end the Tip with a slightly more difficult deal. Take the South cards and see what you make of it.

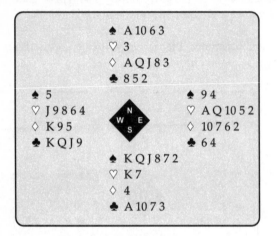

West leads the ♣K against your ambitious contract of 6♠. What is your plan? In particular, how will you play the diamond suit?

Suppose you manage to set up a total of three diamond tricks without surrendering the lead. This will not be good enough to make the contract. Whatever discards you take on the two surplus diamonds, you will be left with two losers in the side suits.

To make the slam, you need to score four diamond tricks. This is possible only if you take a normal diamond finesse, leading low to the queen, and then find that West started with ◇K-x-x. The ◇A and a diamond ruff will bring down West's king and you will score a total of four diamond tricks, allowing you to throw all your club losers. You can then lead a heart towards the king, ruffing your remaining heart if the ♡A proves to be offside.

Tip
14

**Keep the danger
hand off lead**

It often happens that one of the defenders is a 'danger hand'. What does this mean? It means that you may be in trouble if he gains the lead. Perhaps he has some winners to cash; perhaps he can make a potentially damaging lead through a king. A huge area of cardplay, known as Avoidance Play, is aimed at keeping the danger hand off lead. Would you have seen how to do it on the following deal?

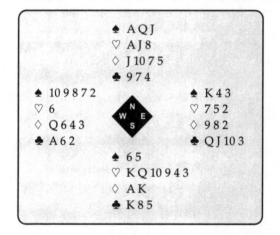

West leads the ♠10 against 4♡ How will you plan the play?

East is the 'danger hand'. If he ever gains the lead, a club switch through your king could prove to be the end of your contract. You have nine top tricks and must aim to score a tenth without allowing East on lead. How can this be done?

You will not fall off your chair when I tell you that finessing the ♠Q at trick one is not the right answer! East will win with the ♠K and switch to the ♣Q, killing the contract. Instead you should win the first trick with dummy's ♠A. You cash the two top diamonds in your hand and return to dummy with the ♡8. Next you lead the ◊J. If East were to cover this card, you would ruff high. You would then draw trumps, ending in the dummy, and enjoy the ◊10 as your tenth trick.

As the cards lie, East will play low on the third round of diamonds. You discard a spade from your hand, killing the link between the defenders, and West wins with the ◊Q.

West will now play a fourth diamond, allowing his partner to ruff the established ◊10. No matter! You overruff in the South hand and return to dummy with a second round of trumps. You then lead the ♠Q. As before, if East covers, you will ruff and return to dummy to enjoy the established winner. If instead East plays low, you will discard a club and set up dummy's ♠J in the process. You will not mind at all if West held the ♠K all along. He is the 'safe hand', the defender who cannot lead through the ♠K. However the cards lie, you will set up a spade as your tenth trick.

The next deal illustrates the same theme. See if you can handle the play correctly.

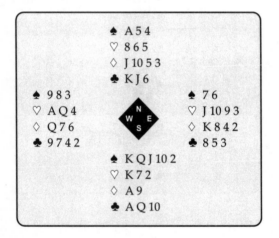

```
              ♠ A 5 4
              ♡ 8 6 5
              ◊ J 10 5 3
              ♣ K J 6
♠ 9 8 3                      ♠ 7 6
♡ A Q 4          N          ♡ J 10 9 3
◊ Q 7 6       W     E       ◊ K 8 4 2
♣ 9 7 4 2        S          ♣ 8 5 3
              ♠ K Q J 10 2
              ♡ K 7 2
              ◊ A 9
              ♣ A Q 10
```

West leads a trump against 4♠. What is your plan?

As before, East is the danger hand, the defender who can switch to a heart through your king if given the chance. You must therefore try to develop a tenth trick without allowing East on lead.

You win the trump lead in your hand and draw trumps with two further rounds, ending in the dummy. You then play a diamond to the nine, finessing into the safe hand. Let's say that West switches to a club now. How would you proceed?

You must win the first round of clubs with your *ace*, leaving two club entries to the dummy. You then cash the ◊A and overtake the ♣10 with the ♣J to return to dummy. Next you lead the ◊J. It makes no difference whatsoever what happens on this trick. If East covers with the ◊K, you will ruff and cross to dummy with the ♣K to score the established diamond trick. If East does not cover, you will discard one of your heart losers, not minding if the safe hand wins the trick. Once again, you will return to dummy with the ♣K to take a discard.

Suppose, on that last deal, the ◊8 and ◊9 had been swapped, leaving this diamond position:

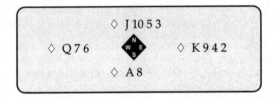

You lead the ◊3 from dummy and East has to insert the ◊9 to beat the contract! If he plays low instead, as most defenders would do, you will insert the ◊8 and make the contract in the same way as before.

Tip

15

**Do not finesse
in trumps when a
ruff is threatened**

Y ou are playing in a suit contract. What is your reaction when a spot card is led and you hold length in that suit in both hands? The opening lead is quite likely to be a singleton. The same is true when a spot-card is led through dummy's main side suit. The defenders are hoping to score a ruff and it is your task to prevent it from happening.

How can you do this? We saw one possibility in the first Tip in this book, on 'disguising a singleton lead'. Another common technique is to vary your normal play in the trump suit. Look at this deal, for example:

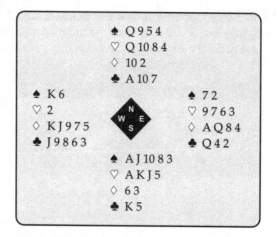

You reach 4♠ and West leads the ♡2. How will you play?

You can see all five honour cards in hearts, so the lead cannot be fourth-best from strength. The odds are high that West has led a singleton. Suppose you win the heart lead with dummy's ten and, taking no special precautions, run the queen of trumps. Not the best! West will win with the trump king and cross to his partner's hand with a diamond. A heart ruff followed by a second diamond winner will put the contract one down.

Since you can afford to lose one trump trick, but not two, you should refuse the finesse in trumps. After winning the heart lead, you should

---

play ace and another trump. When trumps are 2-2, as in the diagram, the contract will be yours. If West started with ♡K-x-x and scores a ruff despite your best efforts, there was nothing you could do about it.

The same argument applies when you are missing five trumps to the queen. Be wary of finessing when this might lead to the loss of two trump tricks. Test yourself on this deal:

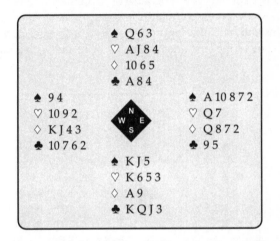

West leads the ♣9 against 4♡. East wins with the ♠A and returns the suit, West following with the ♣4. How will you play?

If you could not afford to lose a trump trick, you would cash the ♡K and then finesse the ♡J. That would be a dangerous play here. If the finesse lost to a doubleton ♡Q, East would give his partner a spade ruff. To remove the risk of losing two trump tricks, you should play the ace and king of trumps instead. Here the ♡Q will fall and you will score an overtrick. If the ♡Q does not fall, you will still make the contract (losing a trump, a diamond and a spade). When West began with ♡Q-10-9-2, you can lead towards dummy's ♡J on the third round.

Suppose South's trumps had been K-10-5-3 instead. You could then have sought an overtrick by cashing dummy's ♡A and finessing the ♡10. You would be 'finessing into the safe hand'. If West won with the ♡Q, he would have no way to cross to East's hand for a spade ruff.

Tip 16   Do not be distracted by a possible finesse

Many a contract is lost because declarer takes a finesse that is not actually necessary. Had the losing honour been a low card instead, not offering any chance of a finesse, declarer might well have spotted the best line of play. We will start with a fairly simple example:

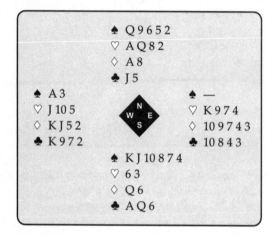

How will you play 4♠ when West leads the ♡J?

There are many thousands of players out there who know only one way to play an ace-queen combination. "Queen, please," they will say. You can see what may happen on this occasion. The finesse loses to East's ♡K and he switches to the ◇10, freeing the defenders' trick in that suit. Declarer cannot avoid an eventual club loser and that will be one down.

There is only one reason for going down on a deal like this. You fail to make a plan! Stop and think for a moment before playing to the first trick and it is easy to see a route to ten tricks. You win with dummy's ♡A and run the ♣J before drawing trumps. No matter that this loses to the ♣K. Suppose West switches to a diamond or plays a heart to East's king, allowing East to switch to a diamond. In both cases you will win with the ◇A and play the ♣A and ♣Q, discarding dummy's diamond loser. With this business behind you, it will be safe to play a trump.

Most declarers would get that one right. I suspect that quite a few might tumble to defeat on the next deal:

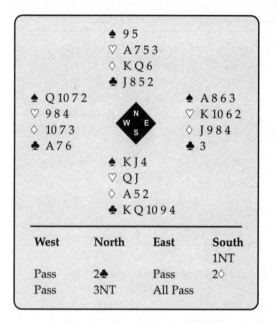

	♠ 9 5		
	♡ A 7 5 3		
	◇ K Q 6		
	♣ J 8 5 2		

West	North	East	South
			1NT
Pass	2♣	Pass	2◇
Pass	3NT	All Pass	

West leads the ♠2 against your contract of 3NT. East wins with the ♠A and returns the ♠3. How will you play?

The original declarer played carelessly. At trick two, he finessed the ♠J. West won with the ♠Q and, sensing that a spade continuation would net only three spades and one club, switched to the ♡9. The contract could no longer be made. If declarer played low from dummy on the heart switch, East would win with the king and switch back to spades, establishing five tricks for the defence. If instead declarer rose with dummy's ♡A, the defenders would eventually score two spades, two hearts and the ♣A.

West's fourth-best lead of the ♠2 should have told declarer that the spades were breaking 4-4. If he had any doubts on the matter, they should have been quelled by East's fourth-best return of the ♠3. The contract was a virtual certainty to make if declarer rose with the ♠K at trick two and established the club suit. No doubt declarer would have seen this, had his spades been K-6-4 instead of K-J-4.

We will end the Tip with a slam deal that once again illustrates the theme that you should not allow your planning to be deflected by the chance to rely on a finesse.

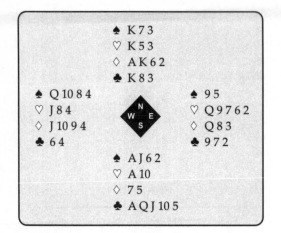

West leads the ◊J against 6♣. How will you play?

If you gave this slam to a dozen declarers of various abilities, you would probably see three different lines of play. The least experienced players would probably draw trumps, cash the ♠K and finesse the ♠J. Much of the time this line would be good enough. They would succeed when East held the ♠Q or the spades divided 3-3.

Players with more experience would know the safety play for three tricks in spades. After drawing trumps, they would play the ♠A and ♠K, planning to lead towards the ♠J on the third round. They would succeed when East held the ♠Q, the spades were 3-3 or West started with a doubleton ♠Q.

To spot the best line, imagine that you did not hold the ♠J. You would then try to ruff a spade in dummy and, indeed, this is the best line. After winning the diamond lead, you should play king, ace and another spade. If spades do not break 3-3, nothing can stop you from ruffing your last spade with dummy's ♣K.

Tip
17

Score your low
trumps to survive
a bad trump break

Y ou can often overcome a bad trump break by scoring the low
trumps in your hand. Would you have seen the winning line here?

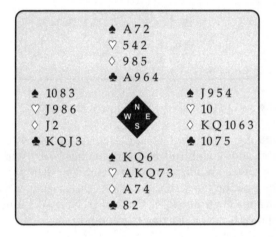

West leads the ♣K against 4♡. How will you play the contract?

If you look at the losers from the South position, you will see an
apparently inescapable two diamond losers and one club loser. You
might then conclude that you will need a 3-2 trump break to make the
game. Think again! You have five potential winners in the side suits. If
you can add five trump tricks to the pot, this will give you a total of ten
tricks. To overcome a 4-1 trump break, you will need to score two club
ruffs in your hand. Since there are only two entries to dummy (the black
aces), you must make full use of them.

The first essential move is to duck the opening lead. You win the club
continuation and ruff a club with the ♡3. When you play the ace and king
of trumps, East shows out on the second round. Is this bad news? Not at
all, it means that your careful early play may be rewarded. You cross to
the ♠A and lead dummy's last club. When East discards, you ruff with
the ♡7 and West has to follow suit. The ace of trumps and two further
winners in spades bring your total to ten tricks.

Here is another deal on the same theme, this time a slam contract:

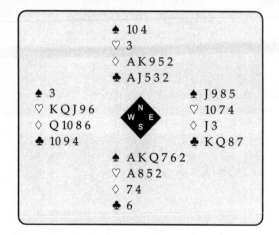

You bid to 6♠ and West leads the ♡K. How will you play?

You win with the ♡A and ruff a heart. After cashing the ♣A, you return to your hand with a club ruff and ruff another heart. When you ruff another club low, both defenders follow suit. You then play the ♠A-K, West showing out on the second round. At this stage you have a heart loser and an apparent trump loser. One down? Not necessarily. You cross to the ◇A and cash the ◇K, leaving this end position:

You lead the ♣J, ruffing with the ♠7, and the ♠Q is your twelfth trick. In the position shown in the diagram, you could equally well lead a diamond. If East chose to ruff, you would discard the heart loser.

Tip
18

Some chance is better than none

When a contract seems to be a poor one, you should not give up. If you can manage to unearth a 10% chance somewhere, this will be a good deal better than following a no-play line. Not only will you make the contract 10% of the time, you will also greatly annoy the defenders by doing so! In this Tip we will look at some contracts that seem unlikely to make when dummy goes down. A chance of success awaits you, nevertheless, if you are willing to look for it. The first deal is relatively easy:

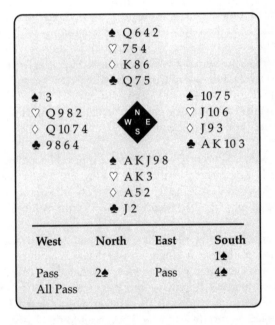

	♠ Q 6 4 2	
	♡ 7 5 4	
	◇ K 8 6	
	♣ Q 7 5	
♠ 3		♠ 10 7 5
♡ Q 9 8 2		♡ J 10 6
◇ Q 10 7 4		◇ J 9 3
♣ 9 8 6 4		♣ A K 10 3
	♠ A K J 9 8	
	♡ A K 3	
	◇ A 5 2	
	♣ J 2	

West	North	East	South
			1♠
Pass	2♠	Pass	4♠
All Pass			

How will you play the spade game when West leads the ◇4?

You have four apparent losers in the side suits. To dispose of one of your red-suit losers, you must set up a winner in clubs. What is the best chance of doing this? If East has the ♣A and ♣K, you can succeed by leading towards the ♣J on the first round. How does the play go?

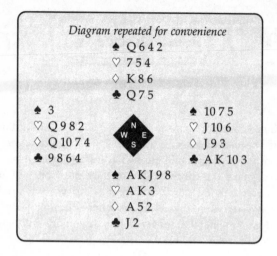

Diagram repeated for convenience

```
                    ♠ Q 6 4 2
                    ♡ 7 5 4
                    ◇ K 8 6
                    ♣ Q 7 5
    ♠ 3                         ♠ 10 7 5
    ♡ Q 9 8 2         N         ♡ J 10 6
    ◇ Q 10 7 4     W   E        ◇ J 9 3
    ♣ 9 8 6 4         S         ♣ A K 10 3
                    ♠ A K J 9 8
                    ♡ A K 3
                    ◇ A 5 2
                    ♣ J 2
```

You win the diamond lead with the ace, conserving your limited entries to the dummy. You then draw trumps in three rounds with the ace, king and jack. At trick five, you cross to dummy with the ◇K. When you lead a club towards your hand, East is powerless. Suppose he rises with the ace or king, cashes a diamond trick and switches to a heart. You will clear your club trick and the ♠Q will allow you to reach the established club winner, discarding a heart on it. If instead East plays low on the first round of clubs, your ♣J will win.

Did that look easy? Perhaps, but there were traps to be avoided. Suppose that you had drawn trumps with the ace, king and queen instead. When you then played a club, East could rise with an honour and remove dummy's last entry (the ◇K) before you had set up a club trick.

Before we move to another deal, how would you have continued if a club to the jack lost to the ace or king with West? The defenders would cash a diamond and switch to a heart, as before. What then? Would you lead towards dummy's ♣Q, hoping to find West with the other missing high honour? It's not a good idea. If West began with the ♣A-K, he would surely have led a club instead of a diamond. On this basis, you should duck the second round of clubs, hoping that East started with ♣A-x or ♣K-x. Some chance is better than none!

The next deal has a similar theme:

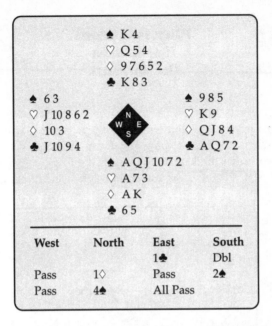

♠ K 4
♡ Q 5 4
◇ 9 7 6 5 2
♣ K 8 3

♠ 6 3
♡ J 10 8 6 2
◇ 10 3
♣ J 10 9 4

♠ 9 8 5
♡ K 9
◇ Q J 8 4
♣ A Q 7 2

♠ A Q J 10 7 2
♡ A 7 3
◇ A K
♣ 6 5

West	North	East	South
		1♣	Dbl
Pass	1◇	Pass	2♠
Pass	4♠	All Pass	

Yes, 3NT would have been easier and North might well have made that bid at his second turn. For the moment, West leads the ♣J against your contract of 4♠. The defenders persist with clubs and you ruff the third round. What now?

It will not be possible to set up and enjoy dummy's diamond suit. Suppose you use dummy's ♠K as an entry to ruff a diamond. Even if the defenders' cards break 3-3, you will not be able to reach the established long cards in the suit. No, you need to score a trick with dummy's ♡Q. How can that be done?

There is not much point in leading a heart towards the queen, hoping that West holds the ♡K. There are only 14 points missing and you have already seen West produce the ♣J. So, unless East has opened on a 10-count he is certain to hold the ♡K. Your best hope is to cash the ♡A and then duck a second round of the suit. It's not particularly likely that East's ♡K is doubleton and will fall on the second round but . . . some chance is better than none!

Tip

19

**Play low from
K-Q-x-x in
the dummy**

W est leads a low club and dummy goes down with ♣K-Q-x-x.
When you have nothing of value in the suit in your own hand,
you may think that it is automatic to play an honour from
dummy. Most of the time, yes, but not always! Look at this deal:

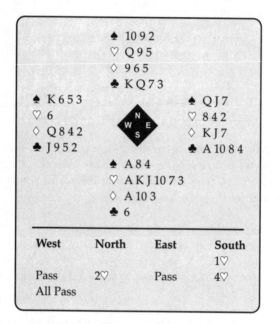

	♠ 10 9 2	
	♡ Q 9 5	
	◇ 9 6 5	
	♣ K Q 7 3	

♠ K 6 5 3		♠ Q J 7
♡ 6	N	♡ 8 4 2
◇ Q 8 4 2	W E	◇ K J 7
♣ J 9 5 2	S	♣ A 10 8 4

	♠ A 8 4	
	♡ A K J 10 7 3	
	◇ A 10 3	
	♣ 6	

West	North	East	South
			1♡
Pass	2♡	Pass	4♡
All Pass			

West leads the ♣2 against 4♡. How will you play?

It may seem natural to play a club honour from the dummy. What is the
point, though? There is not one chance in a thousand that West holds the
♣A. One discard on the clubs will not be much use either, since you will
still have three losers left in spades and diamonds. Try playing low
instead! When the cards lie as in the diagram there is then at least a
chance that East will read his partner for a singleton club. In that case he
will win with the ♣A and you will have two discards – enough for the
contract.

Even when East holds ♣A-J-x-x and wins the first trick with the jack, you have not lost anything. You can still set up one discard by taking a ruffing finesse in clubs later.

Sometimes it is right to play low from dummy's K-Q-x-x because you don't want your right-hand opponent to gain the lead. That's the situation here:

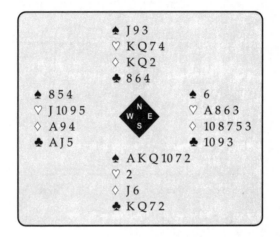

West leads the ♡J against 4♠. How will you play?

Suppose you have switched to auto-pilot ('I'll make a plan later if it proves to be necessary') and you play a heart honour from the dummy at trick one. East wins with the ♡A and will probably switch to the ♣10. This will establish four tricks for the defenders and there will be no way for you to retrieve the situation.

A better idea is to play low from dummy at trick one. East cannot afford to overtake with the ♡A or you will have two discards available on the ♡K-Q. West is left on lead and, as the cards lie, cannot damage you from his side of the table. You will win his return and take a ruffing finesse in hearts. You will then have two discards for your club losers – one on each red suit.

Let's change the deal a little, giving East the ◊A. After winning the first trick with the ♡J, West could then defeat you with a brilliant switch to the ♣5. East's ♣9 would drive out one of your club honours and when he subsequently won with the ◊A he could lead a club through your remaining honour. At least, in that case, the defenders would have had to work for their success. If you cover the opening lead, playing an honour from dummy's heart holding, you make life easy for them.

We will end the Tip by looking at a situation in which you have a chance of setting up two tricks by force, provided you do not waste an honour from dummy's K-Q-x-x at trick one:

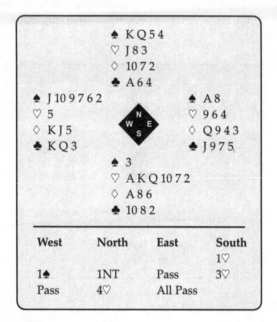

	♠ K Q 5 4		
	♡ J 8 3		
	◇ 10 7 2		
	♣ A 6 4		

West	North	East	South
			1♡
1♠	1NT	Pass	3♡
Pass	4♡	All Pass	

Yes, 3NT might have been a better spot. You end in 4♡, however, and West leads the ♠J. How will you play?

If you cover with one of dummy's honours, you will score six trump tricks and three side-suit winners, going one down. This would be poor play. There is no way that West will lead the ♠J when he holds the ♠A. It is a near certainty that West's spades are headed by the jack-ten and that East has the ♠A. You should therefore duck the first spade, allowing West's ♠J to win.

Let's suppose that West switches to the ♣K at trick two. You will win with dummy's ♣A and ruff a spade. East's ♠A appears, you are pleased to see, and you ruff in the South hand. You can then draw trumps, ending in the dummy, and discard two minor-suit losers on the ♠K-Q.

This sort of ducking play is more familiar in a different guise. Suppose West leads the ♠Q and dummy goes down with ♠K-x-x-x opposite your ♠x-x or ♠x-x-x. You would not commit dummy's king, of course. You would duck twice, attempting to bring down East's ♠A and thereby set up a trick for dummy's ♠K.

S uppose you are defending in the East seat and your partner leads
the ◇A against a contract such as 4♠. If you like the lead you will
encourage a continuation with a high card. ('Yes, yes, I have played
the game before,' you will be saying.) Did you know that you can also
encourage a continuation when you are declarer? Perhaps this is the
situation in the suit that has been led:

West leads the ◇A and East discourages a continuation by playing the ◇5,
his lowest card in the suit. A diamond continuation would suit you, as
declarer, since it would set up your ◇Q. You should therefore 'encourage'
by following with the ◇6. Do you see the effect of this? West will notice
that the ◇3 is missing. He may conclude that East has given him an
encouraging signal from ◇Q-5-3 and continue the suit.

You will meet players who go through their entire bridge careers without
making deceptive plays of this sort. If you discuss the matter with them,
they say: "The defender would never fall for it. It's not worth bothering."
There are two answers to give to such an argument. The first is that
many, many players do fall into such traps. Whenever you create a choice
of plays for them, they will often choose the wrong one. Just as compelling
is the fact that the defenders will never go wrong in such a position if you
do not at least try to fool them.

Suppose you follow woodenly with the ◇3 on the first trick, West will
know that East has played his lowest diamond and is discouraging a
continuation. You have absolutely nothing to lose by following with the
◇6, thereby giving West a losing option.

A further benefit of acquiring a reputation as a tricky declarer is that a
defender may think you are false-carding when you are not. Suppose this

is the diamond position:

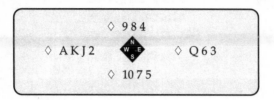

Again West leads the ◊A against your spade game. This time East plays the ◊6, to encourage a diamond continuation, and you follow with the ◊5. If West rates you as an imaginative false-carder, he may say to himself: "I bet old so-and-so is hiding the ◊3. He probably has ◊Q-5-3 and is hoping that I will play another diamond and set up his queen." West may then switch elsewhere, allowing you to discard one or more diamonds at a later stage.

Suppose instead that the defenders at your club get to know that you always follow with your lowest spot-card, as declarer. They will be certain here that East is indeed trying to encourage with his ◊6.

Sometimes, as declarer, you have a choice of two spot cards with which to 'encourage'. Should you always play the higher one? Usually this will be a mistake. You should calculate what holding you are painting for the defender in the East seat. An example will make this clear.

West leads the ♣A against your major-suit game and East discourages with the ♣5. A club continuation would be agreeable and you must choose a card from the South hand to encourage a continuation. Obviously you will 'hide' the ♣2, so that West will place this card with East. Should you follow with the ♣8, though, or the ♣7?

Suppose you follow with the ♣8. West will think along these lines: "If partner held ♣Q-7-5-2 he would have encouraged with the ♣7, choosing his highest available spot card to make the message clear. So, either East holds the ♣7 (and the ♣5 is a discouraging card) or declarer is playing a false card."

When you choose an encouraging card as declarer you should play the lowest card that beats East's signal. Here you should 'cover' East's ♣5 with the ♣7. From West's point of view, East may now be encouraging from ♣Q-5-2.

It's time to look at a full deal where you might employ such a tactic:

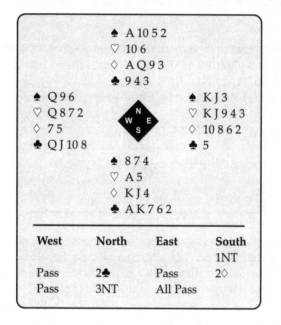

	♠ A 10 5 2		
	♡ 10 6		
	◇ A Q 9 3		
	♣ 9 4 3		

West	North	East	South
			1NT
Pass	2♣	Pass	2◇
Pass	3NT	All Pass	

West leads the ♣Q against 3NT, East following with the ♣5. How will you play the contract?

You have eight tricks on top and the best chance of establishing a ninth trick is in the club suit. What will happen if you win the club lead and return another club, knocking out one of West's stoppers in the suit? West will see his partner show out on the second round of clubs and direct his attention elsewhere, almost certainly to the under-protected heart suit. You will go one down.

A much better idea is to feign weakness in the club suit – allowing West's ♣Q to win. You should also attempt to encourage a club continuation. With this aim in mind, which card should you play from the South hand?

You should 'cover' East's ♣5 with the ♣6, making it look as if East is signalling encouragement from ♣K-5-2 or ♣A-5-2. If instead you follow with the ♣7, West may be suspicious. He will say to himself: "Where is the ♣6? Either East has it and is discouraging a club continuation or South has it and is false-carding."

Play the recommended ♣6 at trick one and the odds are high that West will play another club, looking extremely unhappy when his partner shows out. (Enjoy the moment!) You will win the second club and give West a club trick, setting up the clubs while you still have the heart suit protected.

Now let's consider briefly the situation where you don't like the opening lead at all and would like to dissuade West from a continuation. What should you do? You should 'discourage' with a low card, following exactly the same method used by the defender in the third seat.

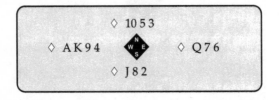

West leads the ◇A against your major-suit game and East plays the ◇7 to encourage a continuation. The situation is fairly hopeless but the best you can do it to follow with the ◇2. It will then at least be possible, from West's point of view, that East is discouraging from ◇J-8-7. If you misguidedly follow with the ◇8 or the ◇J, East's ◇7 will look even more encouraging than it already does.

Tip
21

Discover if you can afford a safety play

T he best way to play a particular holding in a suit may vary according to how many tricks you need from it. Suppose this is your trump suit:

If you cannot afford to lose a trump trick, you will finesse the jack on the first round, hoping that West started with ♡K-x.

Now suppose you can afford one trump loser, but not two. You must look for a safety play that maximizes your chance of three tricks from the suit. You should cash the ace on the first round, staving off defeat when East holds a singleton ♡K. If the king does not fall but the ten or nine does, you will choose your play on the second round to catch the situation where the ten or nine was a singleton. Perhaps the suit lies like this:

When the ace drops the nine from East, you will continue with a low card to the queen. West wins with the king but dummy's ♡J-7 will allow you to finesse against the ten on the next round.

In this Tip we will delve a little deeper into the situation, looking at deals where you must determine whether you can afford to take a safety play. You do this by testing the lie of one suit to see how many tricks you will then need from a different suit.

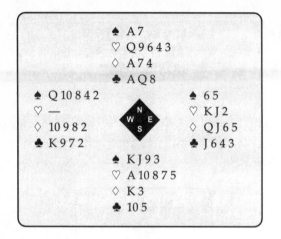

♠ A 7
♡ Q 9 6 4 3
◇ A 7 4
♣ A Q 8

♠ Q 10 8 4 2
♡ —
◇ 10 9 8 2
♣ K 9 7 2

♠ 6 5
♡ K J 2
◇ Q J 6 5
♣ J 6 4 3

♠ K J 9 3
♡ A 10 8 7 5
◇ K 3
♣ 10 5

West leads the ◇10 against 6♡. How will you play?

If you evaluate the loser situation from the South hand, you will see that the two potential spade losers can be ruffed. There are no losers in diamonds and one potential loser in clubs, which might evaporate if the club finesse wins. How many losers can you afford in the trump suit? You don't know yet. It depends on whether you have a club loser!

You cannot tell how to play the trump suit (whether you can afford to make a safety play) until you have tested the club suit. You should win the diamond lead with the ◇K and play a club to the queen immediately, before drawing trumps. When the cards lie as in the diagram, the ♣Q will win. Since you now have no losers in the side suits, you can afford one loser in the trump suit. You should therefore play safe to guard against two trump losers. Can you see what the appropriate safety play is?

At trick three you should lead a low trump towards your hand, finessing the ♡10 if East follows with the ♡2. Here, your finesse of the ten will succeed, West showing out. If the finesse were to lose, to the jack or the king, there would be only one trump still out and you could draw this with the ace when you regained the lead. If instead East had shown out on the first round of trumps, you would have risen with the trump ace and led a second round towards dummy's queen, again restricting your trump losers to one. There would be no problem, of course, if East followed with an honour on the first round.

You get the idea, then. You test the lie of one suit to see if you can afford a safety play in another suit. Test yourself on this deal:

---

52 Great Bridge Tips on Declarer Play

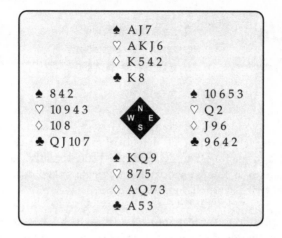

West leads the ♣Q against 6NT. How will you plan the contract?

There are ten tricks on top – eleven if the diamonds break 3-2. The heart suit offers a potential safety play for three tricks, as we will see in a moment. Can you afford to take this safety play? It depends on how the diamonds are breaking.

You should win the club lead and play two rounds of diamonds. When the cards lie as in the diagram, diamonds will break 3-2. You will then need only three heart tricks. Do you know the right safety play?

You should cash the ♡A-K on the first two rounds, planning to lead towards the jack on the third round. In this way you make three tricks not only when the ♡Q is onside or hearts break 3-3. You succeed also when East holds a doubleton (or singleton) queen. Here – wouldn't you know it? – the ♡Q is indeed doubleton offside, so the safety play pays off and you make the contract.

What would happen if the diamonds broke 4-1 instead? Since three heart tricks would bring your total only to eleven, you would abandon the safety play in hearts and finesse the ♡J, hoping to score four heart tricks. If the heart finesse were to lose, that would almost certainly be the end of your contract. What if the heart finesse were to win? You would then have eleven top tricks and there would be the chance of a squeeze if the same defender held four cards in both the red suits. If you are familiar with squeeze technique, you will understand that you should duck a round of clubs to rectify the count. You can then cash the black-suit winners, squeezing a defender with lengths in both red suits.

Use the short trumps to protect against a force

S uppose you hold five trumps and one of the defenders holds four trumps against you. The defenders may then attack your trump length by leading their own strongest suit, forcing you to ruff. This style of defence is known as 'playing a forcing game'. If they can force you to ruff twice, you will lose trump control.

What can you do to protect yourself against such a hostile attack? One valuable technique is to use the shorter trump holding, usually in dummy, to guard against the force. That's what happens on this deal:

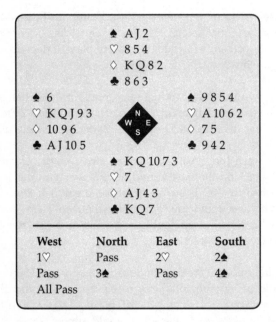

	♠ A J 2	
	♡ 8 5 4	
	◊ K Q 8 2	
	♣ 8 6 3	
♠ 6		♠ 9 8 5 4
♡ K Q J 9 3		♡ A 10 6 2
◊ 10 9 6		◊ 7 5
♣ A J 10 5		♣ 9 4 2
	♠ K Q 10 7 3	
	♡ 7	
	◊ A J 4 3	
	♣ K Q 7	

West	North	East	South
1♡	Pass	2♡	2♠
Pass	3♠	Pass	4♠
All Pass			

West leads the ♡K against your spade game and continues the suit. You ruff with the ♠3 and play the ace and king of trumps to see how the suit breaks. If both defenders were to follow, you would draw the last trump and make the contract easily. When the cards lie as in the diagram, West will show out on the second round of trumps. What now?

If your next move is to draw East's remaining trumps, you will go down.

Five spades and four diamonds will bring your total to only nine. When you attempt to score a club trick, the defenders will grab the ♣A immediately and score several heart tricks.

Instead you must leave the ♠J in dummy, where it will act as a sentinel against the defenders' heart suit. At trick five you lead the ♣K from your hand. West wins with the ace and these cards are still to be played:

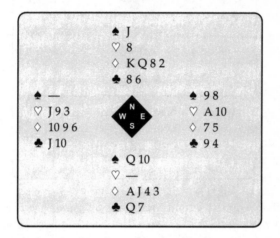

What should you do when West plays a heart to East's ace?

If you ruff, you will lose control and go at least one down. Instead you should throw the ♣7 from your hand. This costs you nothing because you were expecting to lose a club trick anyway. If the defenders play yet another heart, this will cause no damage. You will ruff in the short-trump hand, with dummy's ♠J. You can then cross to your hand with the ◊A, draw East's remaining two trumps and claim the contract.

It's an important technique, one that you will use many times in your bridge career. You discard losers from your hand until you can ruff with the shorter trump holding in dummy.

Here is another example, this time played in a 4-3 trump fit. You're not interested in that because you never play in a 4-3 fit? Perhaps you should try it!

```
                    ♠ J 7 6
                    ♡ K 3 2
                    ◇ A J 4 2
                    ♣ A K Q
    ♠ A K Q 10 4              ♠ 8 5 3
    ♡ 8 6             N        ♡ 10 9 7 5
    ◇ K 8 5       W     E      ◇ Q 10 9 3
    ♣ 8 6 2          S         ♣ 9 7
                    ♠ 9 2
                    ♡ A Q J 4
                    ◇ 7 6
                    ♣ J 10 5 4 3
```

West	North	East	South
	1◇	Pass	1♡
1♠	Dbl	Pass	2♡
Pass	4♡	All Pass	

North's double on the second round was a Support Double, showing a hand of any strength with just three-card heart support. How would you play the heart game when West starts with three top spades?

If you ruff the third spade, reducing yourself to three trumps, you will go down (even if trumps are 3-3, because the club suit is blocked). It is better to discard a diamond from your hand, leaving West on lead. Suppose he switches to a diamond at trick four. What then?

You must overcome the blockage in clubs. After winning the diamond switch with the ace, you draw two rounds of trumps with the ace and king. You then cash the ♣A-K, pleased to see both defenders follow suit. When you play a trump to the queen West shows out. You continue with the ♡J, throwing the blocking ♣Q in dummy. Now you can cash three more club tricks in your hand and the contract is yours.

The play is similar if West plays a fourth spade instead of switching to diamonds. You ruff low in the dummy and East cannot hurt you by overruffing. You will overruff in the South hand, cross to the ♡K and cash two top clubs. You will then draw trumps in two more rounds and again discard the blocking club honour in dummy. If instead East chooses to discard on the fourth spade, you will proceed as before.

Tip 23   Discard winners to avoid a ruff

It is a blind spot among some players that it can be beneficial to discard winning cards when a ruff is threatened. Look at this deal, for example:

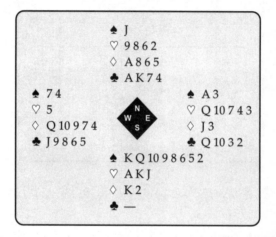

```
                    ♠ J
                    ♡ 9 8 6 2
                    ◇ A 8 6 5
                    ♣ A K 7 4
    ♠ 7 4                          ♠ A 3
    ♡ 5                            ♡ Q 10 7 4 3
    ◇ Q 10 9 7 4                   ◇ J 3
    ♣ J 9 8 6 5                    ♣ Q 10 3 2
                    ♠ K Q 10 9 8 6 5 2
                    ♡ A K J
                    ◇ K 2
                    ♣ —
```

West leads the ♡5 against your small slam in spades. How will you play?

The original declarer played with commendable speed but was one down within ten seconds. He captured East's ♡Q with the ace and led the king of trumps. East won with the trump ace and gave his partner a heart ruff. One down!

There was no certainty that West's ♡5 was a singleton but any spot-card lead against a slam carries this risk. More to the point, there is a virtually foolproof way to overcome such a danger. Before playing on trumps, you should cross to the ◇A and play dummy's two club winners, discarding the king and jack of hearts. You continue with the trump king to East's ace and can now ruff the second round of hearts high in the South hand. You then draw the remaining trumps and claim the contract. Such a play is not in the least bit difficult but it is amazing how careless some players can be.

Here is a slightly trickier deal on the same theme:

```
                    ♠ Q 9 2
                    ♡ J 4
                    ◊ A K Q 5
                    ♣ A K 7 4
   ♠ 7 5                              ♠ A 6
   ♡ K 10 7 6 3 2        N            ♡ Q 8
   ◊ 10 8 7 4         W     E         ◊ J 9 3 2
   ♣ 8                   S            ♣ 10 6 5 3 2
                    ♠ K J 10 8 4 3
                    ♡ A 9 5
                    ◊ 6
                    ♣ Q J 9
```

West	North	East	South
	1♣	Pass	1♠
Pass	2NT	Pass	3♠
Pass	4♣	Pass	4♡
Pass	4NT	Pass	5♡
Pass	6♠	All Pass	

West leads the ♣8 against your contract of 6♠. How will you play the contract?

We noted on the previous deal that a spot-card lead against a slam should ring the 'singleton' warning bell. This is particularly true when the lead is in a suit that you or your partner has bid. Here North opened the bidding with 1♣ and West's lead in that suit carries a higher chance than normal of being a singleton. What can you do about it?

You win the opening club lead in your hand and play three rounds of diamonds, discarding your remaining clubs. With the risk of a club ruff averted, you lead a trump. The slam cannot be beaten. East wins with the trump ace and you capture his return, ruffing high if he plays a club. You can then draw trumps and discard your two heart losers on the ♣A-K, which survive in the dummy.

Was there a risk in playing three rounds of diamonds before drawing trumps? Yes, of course, but it was less than the risk that the opening lead was a singleton and that East would win with the ace of trumps and deliver a club ruff.

Tip 24

Finesse the overcaller's partner for the trump queen

Suppose there has been no enemy bidding and you end in some high contract with a trump holding of ♠A-9-8-3 facing ♠K-J-10-6-2. Will you play for the drop or finesse one of the defenders for the queen? Often there are tactical reasons for playing the suit in one way or another. That is the case on this deal:

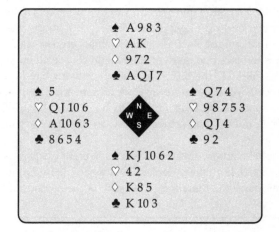

West leads the ♡Q against 4♠ and you win with dummy's ♡A. How will you play the contract?

Suppose you follow the 'eight ever, nine never' guideline, playing the ace and king of trumps. The trump queen will not fall and when you turn to clubs, hoping to discard a diamond, East will ruff the third round with the ♠Q. A diamond switch will then beat the contract.

A better way to play the trump suit is to cash the ace and finesse the jack on the second round. Here the finesse will win. You can draw the last trump and discard one of your diamond losers to score an overtrick. You wouldn't mind at all if the trump finesse lost, because the safe (West) hand would be on lead. He could not attack diamonds productively from his side of the table and you would eventually throw one of your diamonds on the fourth round of clubs.

What is the situation when there are no such tactical considerations present? You cash the ace, two spot cards appearing and lead a second round, East playing the remaining spot card. Should you finesse or not? These are the relative odds:

Playing for the drop: 52%
Finessing on the second round: 48%

So, when you hold nine cards missing the queen there is not much in it.

Now suppose that one of the opponents has overcalled. What difference does this make to the odds? You hear some players saying: "West had bid, so he was more likely to hold the missing queen." There is not much sense in that. A doubleton queen in the opponent's suit is not worth very much when you end up playing the contract. It is more of a defensive value, one that might incline you against an overcall. Of more importance is the fact that an overcaller suggests considerable length in the suit he has bid. He therefore has less space in his hand for length in your trump suit. When you are missing four trumps to the queen, the overcaller is more likely than normal to hold a singleton trump. It is usually right to finesse the partner of the overcaller for the trump queen.

These are the relevant figures when you have eight cards missing in the suit of the overcall, both defenders follow low on the first round, and the first defender plays the remaining low card on the second round:

The overcaller's suit breaks	5-3	6-2	7-1
Playing for the drop	46.7%	40.0%	33.3%
Finessing on the second round	53.3%	60.0%	66.7%

Even if the overcall was made only on a five-card suit, which is unlikely at the two-level, the odds favour finessing the overcaller's partner for the trump queen.

Let's see a typical deal, from the 2004 Olympiad match between Italy and the USA, where both declarers followed the advice in this Tip:

```
                    ♠ 9 4
                    ♡ A J 9 4
                    ◇ A 7 3
                    ♣ K 10 5 2
    ♠ K 8 6 5 2                      ♠ Q J 10
    ♡ K 2              N             ♡ Q 8 7 5
    ◇ Q 10 6 5 4    W     E          ◇ 9 8 2
    ♣ 8               S             ♣ Q 9 4
                    ♠ A 7 3
                    ♡ 10 6 3
                    ◇ K J
                    ♣ A J 7 6 3
```

West	North	East	South
Rosenberg	*Bocchi*	*Zia*	*Duboin*
Pass	1♣	Pass	2♣
2♠	Pass	Pass	Dbl
Pass	3♡	Pass	3NT
All Pass			

South's 2♣ was a forcing 'inverted raise'. On lead against 3NT, Rosenberg decided to try his luck with a diamond lead. Duboin won with the ◇J. He then crossed to the ♣K and, guided by West's overcall, finessed the ♣J. The finesse won and he ended with eleven tricks.

At the other table the Italian West chose to overcall 2◇, after the same 1♣ – 2♣ start, and then led a low spade against 3NT. East scored two spade tricks, South holding up the ace, and switched to a diamond. Declarer's main chance of making the contract was to guess the clubs correctly. Once again he was guided by the fact that West had overcalled. He won the diamond switch with the king, crossed to the ♣K and finessed East for the ♣Q to make his game.

Before we move to the next Tip, let's see one more example of a great star following the advice offered in the present one. Well, I promised you a great star. Does Omar Sharif fit the bill? Here he is, facing a world-class Norwegian pair in the 1997 Macallan Invitation Pairs:

```
                    ♠ Q 2
                    ♡ K J 10 5 2
                    ◇ 6 2
                    ♣ 5 4 3 2
  ♠ A 10 8 6                        ♠ 9 7 4 3
  ♡ Q 8 7 6 3         N            ♡ 4
  ◇ J 8 4         W       E        ◇ A K 10 7 5
  ♣ 9                 S            ♣ Q 8 6
                    ♠ K J 5
                    ♡ A 9
                    ◇ Q 9 3
                    ♣ A K J 10 7
```

West	North	East	South
Helness	*Mari*	*Helgemo*	*Sharif*
			1♣
1♡	Pass	Pass	1NT
Pass	3NT	All Pass	

Tor Helness led the ♡6 against 3NT and Sharif won with the ace to keep the entry position fluid. When he cashed the ♣A, both defenders followed low. Since a spade trick would be needed in any case, Sharif continued with a spade to dummy's queen. He then led a club and, guided by West's overcall, finessed the jack. West did indeed show out, so declarer had five club tricks. A finesse of the ♡J succeeded and dummy's ♡K was declarer's ninth trick.

Hearts were known to be 5-1, so East was favourite to hold the ♣Q. Finessing on the second round gave Omar Sharif a 69.1% chance of making five club tricks. Playing for the drop would have been only a 60.9% prospect. This may not seem like much of a difference but, of course, both lines succeed when the ♣Q is singleton, or doubleton in the East hand. Suppose you consider only the situation where both defenders have followed low on the first round and East then follows low on the second round. There is only one card out, the ♣Q. When hearts are known to be 5-1, it is a 59% chance that East has the missing queen and a 41% chance that West has it.

So, be prepared to flout the 'nine never' rule when an opponent has made an overcall. The odds will be in your favour!

Tip
25

Win with a high card to create an entry

In this Tip we will look at situations where you can create an extra entry to dummy by winning the first trick with a higher card than is necessary.

Suppose West leads the ♠6 against 3NT and the spade suit lies like this:

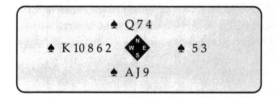

You play low from dummy and East plays the ♠3. If you win with the ♠9 or the ♠J, you will not be able to use the ♠Q as an entry to dummy later. (West will win the second round with the ♠K and you will have to win the third round with the ♠A.) To ensure that the ♠Q is an entry to dummy, you must win the first round with the ♠A. West cannot then prevent you from reaching dummy with the ♠Q.

Let's see this combination in the context of a full deal:

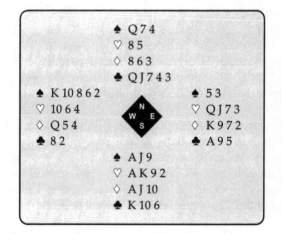

West leads the ♣6 against 3NT, East playing the ♣5. How will you play?

If you win the first trick cheaply, with the ♣9 or ♣J, you will go down. East will hold up the ♣A until the third round and you can wave goodbye to the dummy. Follow the Tip and win the first round with the ♣A. When you clear the clubs, East winning the third round, the defenders are powerless. East can try his luck with a diamond switch but you will play the ◊J and West cannot safely continue the suit when he wins with the ◊Q. You can win any continuation and lead towards the ♣Q, establishing an entry to dummy and the two winning clubs there.

(You would follow the same line with only ◊A-J-9. If the ◊9 lost to West's ◊10 and he persisted with the suit, you would hold up the ◊A until the third round. Unless West began with four or more diamonds, you could still set up the ♣Q as an entry and make the contract. You would lose one spade, two diamonds and one club.)

Let's look at a slightly more difficult setting for this Tip:

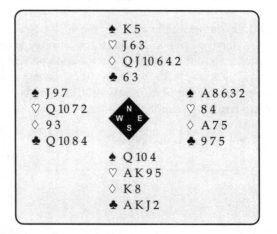

How will you play 3NT when West leads the ♡2?

You must bring in dummy's diamonds. East will hold up the ◊A until your own diamonds are exhausted and you will then need an entry to dummy, in spades or in hearts. If West holds the ♠A, you can reach dummy with dummy's ♠K. This is only a 50% chance, though (45% if you're an unlucky player!). A better idea is to use the ♡J as an entry, since West's lead of the ♡2 suggests that he holds the ♡Q.

You play low from dummy on the first trick and East plays the ♡8. If you win cheaply with the ♡9 you will not be able to reach dummy with the ♡J and the contract will fail. Instead you must win with the ♡A or the ♡K. You clear the diamond suit, East winning the second round. Whether East plays a club or a heart now, you can set up dummy's ♡J as an entry to the long diamonds. All the suits are guarded, so the defenders cannot hurt you.

Sometimes you win with a higher card than is necessary in order to set up a second entry in the suit. That's what happens here:

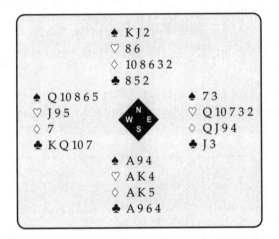

West leads the ♠6 against 3NT. You play low from dummy and East plays the ♠7. How will you play the contract?

All will be easy if diamonds break 3-2 or if East holds a singleton honour in the suit. What if the defenders hold two diamond stoppers, though? You will then need two entries to dummy – one to set up the diamonds and another to reach the long card in the suit.

You should win the first trick with the ♠A, an unnecessarily high card. When you cash the ◊A-K West throws a spade on the second round. East wins the third diamond and switches to a heart, which you win with the ace. Thanks to your unblock of the ♠A at trick one, everything will now go smoothly. You play a spade to the jack and clear the diamonds. You can then win the return and reach the long diamond with the ♠K.

If East had switched to clubs instead of hearts, you would duck one round and win the club continuation, thereby preventing the defenders from scoring three clubs and two diamonds.

Tip 26

Look for an 'extra chance' play

You bid to some high-level contract and – exciting moment – the dummy goes down. Sometimes the contract will be cold. More often than you would like, the contract will offer no play. Most of the time, though, there will be a central line of play that will give you the contract provided the cards lie in a certain way. "Looks like I need East to hold the ace of diamonds," you may say. In such a contract it can pay you to look around for a small extra chance. Once in a while this will rescue you.

The first deal is relatively straightforward but many declarers would go down, not even realising that they should have made the contract:

```
              ♠ A 10 3
              ♡ 10 2
              ◇ A K 8 7 6 4
              ♣ 4 2
♠ J 2                        ♠ K Q 8 6
♡ K 9          N             ♡ Q 8 7 5 3
◇ 10 5 3 2   W   E           ◇ J 9
♣ Q J 10 9 5   S             ♣ 7 6
              ♠ 9 7 5 4
              ♡ A J 6 4
              ◇ Q
              ♣ A K 8 3
```

West	North	East	South
	1◇	Pass	1♡
Pass	2◇	Pass	3NT
All Pass			

How will you play 3NT when West leads the ♣Q?

Suppose you win the club lead and cash the ◇Q. There is only one entry to dummy (the ♠A) and you will make the contract only when diamonds break 3-3. That is not the case on the present lay-out and you will go down.

A better idea, after winning the club lead, is to overtake the ◊Q with dummy's ◊A. You continue with king and another diamond and will now make the contract when one of the defenders holds ◊J-10, ◊J-9 or ◊10-9. When diamonds are 3-3 you will still make the contract, of course. You will score five diamond tricks and four top winners in the other suits.

How much is the 'extra chance' worth on this deal? The chance of a 4-2 diamond break is 48%. There are fifteen possible doubletons and by playing the contract in the recommended way you will succeed when a defender holds three of the fifteen diamond doubletons. You will be adding almost 10% to your chance of making the contract!

See if you can spot the extra chance on this slam hand:

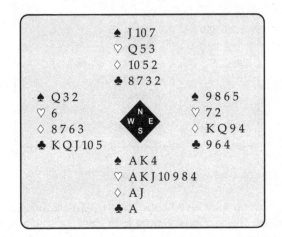

How will you play 6♡ when West leads the ♣K?

The obvious 'main line' is to take a spade finesse, making the slam when East holds the ♠Q. As it happens, the finesse is destined to fail. What 'extra chance' is there?

There is a very worthwhile prospect of developing a second diamond trick. After winning the club lead, you should play the ace of trumps and continue with the jack of trumps, overtaking with dummy's queen. (You save the ♡4, so that you can cross to dummy's ♡5 later, if need be.) You then lead a diamond from dummy, planning to insert the ◊J if East follows low. When East holds both missing diamond honours, which is around a 24% chance, you will score two diamond tricks, whether or not East elects to play an honour on the first round. There is also a tiny chance that East will hold ◊K-x or ◊Q-x, in which case his honour will fall under your ace on the second round, setting up dummy's ◊10.

If no luck comes from the extra-chance play in diamonds, nothing has been lost! You will lead the ♡4 to dummy's ♡5 and take the spade finesse, still making the slam when East holds the ♠Q.

On the next deal, the 'extra chance' is smaller and perhaps more difficult to spot:

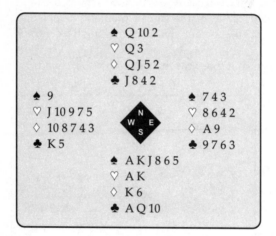

How will you play 6♠ when West leads the ♡J?

Your first reaction may be: "Looks like I need East to hold the king of clubs." Indeed, this is almost certain to be the case. There is, however, a small extra chance in diamonds. After winning the heart lead, you cross to dummy with a trump and lead a low diamond to the king. When the king wins, you continue with the ◊6, playing the ◊5 from dummy (since one discard on the diamonds is no use to you). The ◊A appears from a sad-looking East and the contract is yours. When East switches to a club, you rise with the ace and draw trumps, ending in the dummy. Away go your two club losers on the ◊Q-J and twelve tricks are yours.

The deals are coming thick and fast! See if you can spot the 'extra chance' on this slam contract:

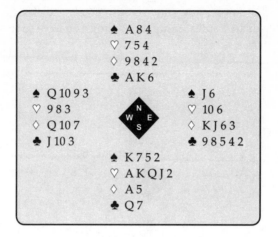

How will you play 6♡ when West leads the ♣J?

Your main chance is that spades will break 3-3. That will happen only 36% of the time. Can you see any way to make the slam when the spades break 4-2?

If the defender with the doubleton spade holds only two trumps, you can engineer a spade ruff. You will need to draw precisely two rounds of trumps before playing the third and fourth rounds of spades. How can you arrange this?

Suppose you win the club lead and draw two rounds of trumps immediately. That's no good. The defender who wins the third round of spades will either be able to draw dummy's last trump or (if he does not hold the last trump) give his partner a spade ruff. Correct technique is to draw just one round of trumps and then to duck the first round of spades. You were always going to lose one spade trick and it makes sense to do so when the defenders cannot do any damage with their return.

Let's say that East wins the first round of spades and switches to a diamond. You win with the ace and draw a second round of trumps. Your next move is to cash the ♠A and the ♠K. If spades break 3-3, you will simply draw the last trump and claim the contract. When the cards lie as in the diagram, your 'extra chance' will pay off. East began with only two spades but he cannot ruff or overruff because he does not hold the last trump. Bad luck for him and good luck for you!

The next deal is similar in a way, because you must play for an 'extra chance' while there is still a trump out. Would you have spotted the best line?

```
                    ♠ K 5 3
                    ♡ A 9 6
                    ◇ K Q 5 4 2
                    ♣ Q 2
  ♠ 8 7 2                          ♠ 9 6
  ♡ Q J 10            N            ♡ K 8 4 2
  ◇ J 10 7 6      W       E        ◇ 9
  ♣ K 9 8             S            ♣ A 10 7 5 4 3
                    ♠ A Q J 10 4
                    ♡ 7 5 3
                    ◇ A 8 3
                    ♣ J 6
```

West	North	East	South
			1♠
Pass	2◇	Pass	2♠
Pass	4♠	All Pass	

West leads the ♡Q and you win with the dummy's ♡A, noting that you have two heart losers and two club losers. What can you do about it?

The 'main chance' is that diamonds will break 3-2. You can then simply draw trumps and run the diamond suit, scoring an easy overtrick. Can you see an 'extra chance' when diamonds do not break 3-2?

You should draw just two rounds of trumps with the ace and queen, both defenders following. Now you play the ◇A and the ◇K. If the diamond suit breaks 3-2, well and good. You will draw the last trump and cash the remaining diamonds. When diamonds break 4-1 and the defender with the singleton diamond does not hold the last trump, you can rescue yourself! You cash a third diamond winner and ruff a diamond. You then cross to the ♠K, drawing West's last trump, and discard a loser on the thirteenth diamond.

The recommended line offers a substantial extra chance. When a defender holds only one diamond, putting your contract at risk, there is a full 27% chance that he will hold exactly two trumps.

Tip 27   Retain the ace to avoid a blockage

Sometimes you have enough tricks for your contract but it is difficult to untangle them. Suppose you hold ♣A-K opposite ♣Q-10-6-4. You have three top tricks and a fourth if the ♣J falls in three rounds. Since the suit is blocked, you will need to cash the ace and king, and then cross to the other hand in a different suit. This much is obvious but the need to unblock the ace-king may cause a problem elsewhere. Would you have seen the solution on the following deal?

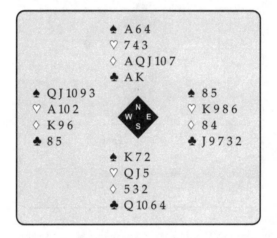

West leads the ♠Q against 3NT. How will you play the contract?

Suppose you win the spade lead in the South hand and finesse the ◊Q. You have no entry to repeat the diamond finesse. If you concede a diamond trick, to set up the suit, you will then have no entry to your ♣Q. You will score four diamonds, two clubs and two spades. One down!

You should win the first round of spades with dummy's ace, saving the ♠K as an entry to reach the ♣Q later. You then unblock the ♣A-K. Since you have stripped dummy of the spade and club entries, you must make sure that you leave the ◊A intact, as an entry to reach the eventually established cards in diamonds. You continue by leading the ◊Q from dummy. If one of the defenders wins this card, you will easily succeed, scoring four diamonds, three clubs and the ♠A-K. If instead the ◊Q is allowed to win, you will continue with the ◊J. When diamonds break 3-2, the defenders will have to take their ◊K on the second round or never score a trick with the card. Again you will have nine tricks. The only problem will arise when a defender has ◊K-x-x-x and holds up the ◊K twice. In that case you will have to lead a heart towards your honours, with various chances remaining.

Test yourself on another deal with the same theme:

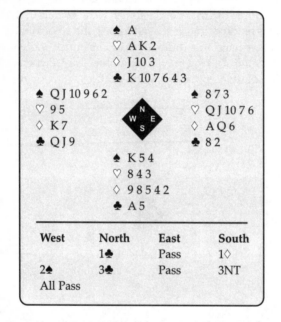

	♠ A		
	♡ A K 2		
	◊ J 10 3		
	♣ K 10 7 6 4 3		
♠ Q J 10 9 6 2		♠ 8 7 3
♡ 9 5		♡ Q J 10 7 6
◊ K 7		◊ A Q 6
♣ Q J 9		♣ 8 2
	♠ K 5 4		
	♡ 8 4 3		
	◊ 9 8 5 4 2		
	♣ A 5		

West	North	East	South
	1♣	Pass	1◊
2♠	3♣	Pass	3NT
All Pass			

How will you play 3NT when West leads the ♠Q to dummy's bare ♠A?

Suppose your next move is to play ace and another club. The clubs will divide 3-2, giving you an apparent nine tricks on top, but you will have no entry to the ♣K. The defenders will lock you in the dummy and eventually claim four tricks in the red suits to put you one down.

The only way to make the contract is to lead a low club from dummy at trick two and to play the ♣5 from your hand. Do you see the point of this? You establish the club suit and at the same time retain the ♣A as an entry to the South hand. It will do West no good now to switch to the ♡9. You can win in the dummy, cross to the ♣A to score your ♠K, and then return to dummy to cash the remaining winners there.

Tip

28

**Look for
the bad break
that can hurt you**

It often happens that a contract is virtually cold, with just one bad break that might hurt you. In that situation you must direct all your attention to finding a line that will survive the hostile break. See if you can spot the answer on this deal:

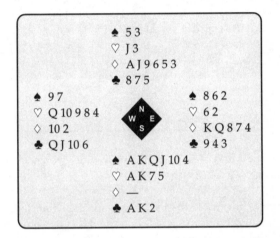

```
              ♠ 5 3
              ♡ J 3
              ◇ A J 9 6 5 3
              ♣ 8 7 5
♠ 9 7                        ♠ 8 6 2
♡ Q 10 9 8 4     N          ♡ 6 2
◇ 10 2        W    E         ◇ K Q 8 7 4
♣ Q J 10 6       S          ♣ 9 4 3
              ♠ A K Q J 10 4
              ♡ A K 7 5
              ◇ —
              ♣ A K 2
```

West leads the ♣Q against your contract of 6♠ and you win with the ♣A. How will you plan the play?

If the hearts break 4-3, you can cash the ♡A-K and reach dummy with a heart ruff. You can then discard one of your remaining losers on the ◇A and move happily to the next deal. When hearts break 5-2, as in the diagram, there will be a different and less happy end to the story. East will overruff dummy on the third round of hearts and this will cost you two tricks. Not only do you lose the ruff, you also lose the entry to dummy's ◇A. Two down!

The 'bad break that can hurt you' here is a 5-2 heart break. What can you do about it? There is no certain safety play but you can halve the chance of defeat by leading a low heart towards the jack at trick two. When West holds the ♡Q you will set up the ♡J as a second-round entry to the dummy and its precious ◇A. You will then be able to draw trumps and claim the slam. What will happen if the ♡J loses to the ♡Q in the East hand? Nothing has been lost! You will win East's return, cash the ♡A and try to ruff your remaining heart loser on the third round of the suit. You will still make the slam if the defenders' hearts were 4-3 all along.

Here is another deal where a bad break may cause your downfall:

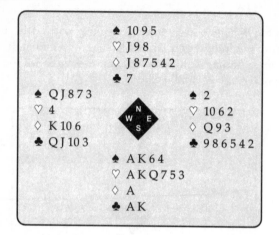

You arrive in 6♡ and West leads the ♣Q, which you win with the ♣A. How will you play the slam?

If spades break no worse than 4-2, you can make the slam easily. After discarding one of dummy's spades on the ♣K, you could cash the two top spades and score at least one spade ruff in the dummy. Suppose you embark on this line when the cards lie as in the diagram. Disaster! East will ruff the ♠K on the second round. You would survive if he had started with only two trumps – you could then draw his remaining trump and ruff your two spade losers. With East still holding ♡10-6, you will go down.

What else can you try? Suppose you cash the ♠A and cross to dummy with the ♡J to lead a spade towards your hand. That's no good either. East will decline to ruff the second spade, letting you score the ♠K. When you throw a spade on the ♣K and ruff a third round of spades with dummy's ♡9, East will overruff and remove dummy's last trump.

To make the slam you should draw one round of trumps, to check that trumps are not 4-0. You then cash your second high club, discarding a spade from dummy. After playing the ♠A you duck a round of spades. Nothing can then prevent you from ruffing your remaining spade loser with dummy's ♡J.

Tip
29

Win the first round to block the defenders' suit

W hen you have the ace of the suit that has been led against no-trumps, it is usually right to hold it up, to exhaust the holding of one of the defenders. Not always! Sometimes you can block the defenders' suit by taking the ace on the first round. Would you find the right play here?

```
                ♠ A Q J 3
                ♡ K J 6 2
                ◇ A J
                ♣ 9 6 4
 ♠ 8 7                        ♠ 10 9 5 4 2
 ♡ A 9 4          N           ♡ 10 8 7 3
 ◇ K 10 8 4 3   W   E         ◇ Q 6
 ♣ Q 10 2          S          ♣ 8 5
                ♠ K 6
                ♡ Q 5
                ◇ 9 7 5 2
                ♣ A K J 7 3
```

West leads the ◇4 against 3NT. How would you plan the play?

Since West's diamonds may be headed by the king-queen, some declarers would try their luck with dummy's ◇J. It is easy to see what would happen next. East would win with the ◇Q and return the ◇6 to dummy's ace, clearing the suit. Whether declarer attempted to set up two extra tricks from the hearts or the clubs, he would then go down.

Instead you should rise with the ◇A at trick one. Since most defenders would lead an honour, rather than a low card, from ◇K-Q-10-x-x, East is marked with the king, queen or ten. If he retains the king or queen, it will block the suit. If instead he unblocks the king or queen under the ace, your remaining ◇9-7-5 (opposite dummy's bare ◇J) will act as a stopper in the suit. You have seven top tricks and the cleanest way to create two more is by knocking out the ♡A.

The other possibility is that East began with ◊10-x:

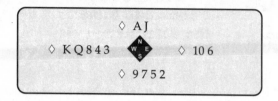

◊ A J

◊ K Q 8 4 3   ◊ 10 6

◊ 9 7 5 2

West leads the ◊4 and a finesse of the ◊J would have succeeded in this case. You play correctly by rising with the ◊A, however, and the defenders can take only two tricks in the suit. West must play an honour on the second round, to capture dummy's jack, and this also picks up East's ◊10 (if he retained it at trick one). Your ◊9-7 is then promoted into a stopper. So, on the assumption that West would have led the king from ◊K-Q-10-x-x, you are assured of success by rising with the ace.

There are several other situations where you should rise with the ace on the first round. Let's see a couple more:

♠ K 10 4
♡ A 4
◊ 10 9 8 6
♣ K 9 5 3

♠ 8 5 3   ♠ J 9 6 2
♡ K J 9 7 2   ♡ Q 8
◊ K 5   ◊ 7 3 2
♣ J 8 2   ♣ Q 10 6 4

♠ A Q 7
♡ 10 6 5 3
◊ A Q J 4
♣ A 7

West leads the ♡7 against 3NT. If you play low from dummy, you will go down. East will win with the ♡Q and clear the heart suit. When the diamond finesse fails, the defenders will have five tricks.

Since West would not have led the ♡7 when his hearts were topped by the K-Q-J, East will have a doubleton honour in the dangerous case when hearts break 5-2. You should therefore rise with the ♡A at trick one. The diamond finesse fails, but the defenders can score only two heart tricks, whether or not East chose to unblock the ♡Q under dummy's ace.

The same play can work well when your holding is headed by the nine:

♡ A 4

♡ K J 8 6 3   ♡ Q 10

♡ 9 7 5 2

West leads the ♡6 against 3NT. If West held any three of the four missing honours (K-Q-J, K-Q-10, K-J-10, or Q-J-10), he would normally lead an honour rather than a low card. You can therefore assume that in the dangerous 5-2 break case East's doubleton contains two honours. Rise with the ♡A and East's remaining honour will block the suit.

Finally, here is a variant of the deal that we saw first:

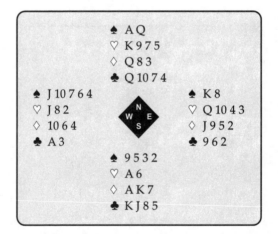

♠ A Q
♡ K 9 7 5
◇ Q 8 3
♣ Q 10 7 4

♠ J 10 7 6 4   ♠ K 8
♡ J 8 2   ♡ Q 10 4 3
◇ 10 6 4   ◇ J 9 5 2
♣ A 3   ♣ 9 6 2

♠ 9 5 3 2
♡ A 6
◇ A K 7
♣ K J 8 5

West leads the ♣6 against 3NT. You have six top tricks and can establish three more by knocking out the ♣A. The only problem is to avoid the loss of four spades and one club. If you finesse the ♠Q at trick one, as at least half of the world's players would, you will go down. East will win and clear the suit. You would survive if East held the ♣A but, no, West wins the first round of clubs and cashes three more spade tricks.

Since West is unlikely to have led low from ♠K-J-10-x-x, you can expect East to hold ♠K-x, ♠J-x or ♠10-x in the dangerous 5-2 case. To guard against the ♠K-x possibility you must rise with the ♠A at trick one. You will then be safe whichever spade honour East has and whichever defender holds the ♣A.

Tip

30

**Cover the lead
to set up a
second-round finesse**

When you are defending, it can be extremely difficult to decide whether to 'cover an honour with an honour'. In my earlier book, *52 Great Bridge Tips*, I suggested that it is wrong for a defender to cover, more often than not. That's because declarer would not usually lead an honour unless he could afford (indeed, would welcome) a cover. The situation is less tricky when you are declarer and have to decide whether to cover the opening lead in the dummy. Since you can see all the cards at your disposal, it should be easy to calculate the best play. Nevertheless, many players go wrong in this situation. Look at this deal:

	♠ K 10 3	
	♡ K 8 3	
	◇ 10 8 6 2	
	♣ A Q 7	
♠ 9 5 4 2		♠ 6
♡ 10 6	N	♡ A J 7 5 4
◇ Q 7 5	W E	◇ A K 9 4
♣ 10 9 6 5	S	♣ J 3 2
	♠ A Q J 8 7	
	♡ Q 9 2	
	◇ J 3	
	♣ K 8 4	

West	North	East	South
		1♡	1♠
Pass	2♡	Pass	2NT
Pass	4♠	All Pass	

East can beat the alternative contract of 3NT with a sharp defence. (He wins the ♡10 lead and switches to ace and another diamond, allowing West to win and play a third round of diamonds through dummy's ◇10-8.) How will you play 4♠ when West leads the ♡10?

Suppose you play low in the dummy, as many declarers would. East has no reason to place his partner with a singleton heart and will doubtless let the ♡10 run to your queen. There will then be no way to avoid two losers in each red suit. To make the contract, you must cover the ♡10 with dummy's ♡K. East wins with the ♡A but you now have a ♡Q-9 tenace sitting over East's ♡J. You will lose only one heart trick and make the contract. It would be a pity to go down when West has made the only opening lead to give you a chance!

Covering was obvious on that deal because the ♡10 lead marked East with the ♡J. The same play would be right even if West led the ♡J. That's because East's opening bid in hearts makes him more likely than West to hold the ♡10. Suppose the situation is different:

		♠ K 10 3		
		♡ K 8 3		
		◇ 9 8 6 2		
		♣ A Q 7		
♠ 9 5 2				♠ 6 4
♡ J 10 6		**N**		♡ A 7 5 4
◇ A Q 5	**W**		**E**	◇ K 10 7 4
♣ 10 9 6 5		**S**		♣ J 3 2
		♠ A Q J 8 7		
		♡ Q 9 2		
		◇ J 3		
		♣ K 8 4		

West	North	East	South
			1♠
Pass	2◇	Pass	2♠
Pass	4♠	All Pass	

West leads the ♡J. How will you play the spade game?

It would still be right to cover if West held ♡J-x. However, such a lead is one of the worst in the game. It is much more likely that West has led from ♡J-10-x or ♡J-10-x-x. You should therefore play low from dummy, preserving the ♡K-8 tenace over West's ♡10. Whether or not East plays the ♡A, you will be able to catch West's ♡10 with a finesse and make the contract. Once again, West will have made the only opening lead to give you a chance!

A finesse is usually a 50-50 prospect. If it wins, you gain a trick. If it loses, you don't. In this Tip we will look at an unusual type of finesse where you will gain a trick whether or not the finesse wins. How can that be possible? Because in the case where the finesse loses you arrange for the defender to be endplayed. Let's see a full-deal example of this:

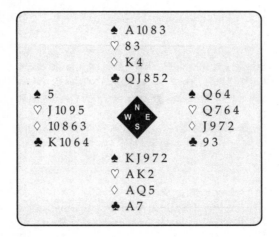

You reach the respectable contract of 6♠ and West leads the ♡J. How will you plan the play?

You can go down only if you lose a trick to both the ♠Q and the ♣K. To prevent this from happening, you begin by eliminating the red suits. You will then take a trump finesse into the West hand at a moment where he will be endplayed if the finesse loses.

How does the play go? You win the heart lead and cash the ♠A. You then play three rounds of diamonds, throwing a heart from dummy. Both defenders follow to the second top heart and you ruff your last heart with the ♠8, giving you some protection against an overruff by East.

The preliminaries have been safely negotiated and you are now in dummy with these cards remaining:

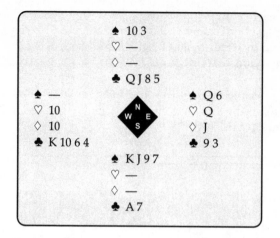

You lead the ♠3 and East follows with the ♠6. Should you finesse or play for the drop? The answer is that you can guarantee the contract by finessing the ♠J. When the cards lie as in the diagram, the finesse will win and you will have twelve tricks. Suppose the trump finesse lost to an original ♠Q-x with West. He would be endplayed, forced to lead a club or to give you a ruff-and-discard.

What if East had shown out on the second round of trumps? You would then insert the ♠J, losing to West's ♠Q. You could then return to dummy with the ♠10 to take the club finesse for the contract.

Here is a slightly more difficult example of the technique:

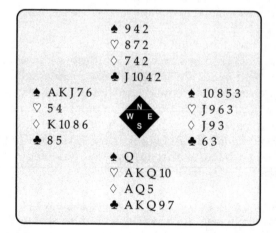

West leads the ♠A-K against 5♣. You ruff the second spade with the ♣A, saving your two trump spot-cards to reach dummy later. You cross to dummy's ♣J and ruff dummy's last spade with the ♣K, eliminating that suit. You then cash the ace and king of hearts, both defenders following with low spot cards.

When you return to dummy with the ♣10, you are pleased to see both defenders following suit. The contract is now guaranteed. This is the position you have reached:

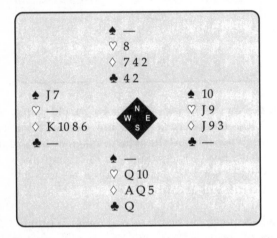

The moment has come moment for the 'cannot lose' finesse. You lead dummy's ♡8, East following with the ♡9, and finesse the ♡10. When the cards lie as in the diagram, the finesse will win. You can discard one of dummy's diamonds on the ♡Q, concede one diamond trick and eventually ruff a diamond in dummy for your eleventh trick.

Suppose West had started with ♡J-5-4 and the third-round heart finesse had lost. You would still make the contract. West would have two losing options. He could return a diamond into your tenace, allowing you to score the queen and ace. You could then discard dummy's last diamond on the ♡Q and ruff your last diamond in dummy. Alternatively, West could return a spade, giving you a ruff-and-discard. You would throw a diamond from dummy and ruff in your hand. The ♡Q would allow you to throw a second diamond from dummy and you would ruff both your diamond losers to make the contract.

Look back to the end diagram. Even if East had shown out on the third heart, you would be safe. You would win the third heart with the queen and throw West on lead with a fourth round of hearts, throwing a diamond from dummy. Again West's return would give you the contract.

**Duck a round
of trumps to
control the hand**

S ometimes you have to lose a trick in the trump suit, or may lose a
trick there if the suit breaks badly. In such a situation it may pay
you to lose the very first round of trumps, rather than a later round.
Why is that? There are various reasons. Let's start with perhaps the most
important one – that you want to have a trump left in dummy when the
defenders take their trump trick. Here is a typical illustration:

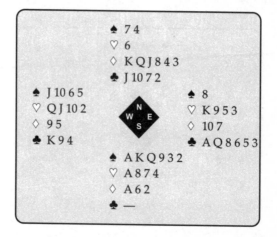

With a big fit in two suits, a grand slam would have been a reasonable
venture. As it happens, you come to a halt in 6♠. How will you tackle this
contract when West leads the ♡Q?

You win the first trick with the ♡A. What will you do next: ruff a heart
or draw a round of trumps? If you succumb to either of these temptations
you will go down! Dummy's diamond suit will allow you to discard
your three heart losers, so there is no need to ruff a heart. If trumps break
3-2, you have thirteen tricks on top. You must therefore consider how to
safeguard the small slam against a 4-1 trump break. Any ideas?

If you have to surrender a trump trick, this must be done at a time when
the defenders cannot cash any heart tricks. That moment is already upon
you! You should duck the very first round of trumps. What can the
defenders do when they win this trick? Absolutely nothing. If they play

another heart, you can ruff in dummy. On any other return you will win, draw trumps and run the diamond suit.

Look back at the full deal and make sure you realise why any other line of play will end in failure. If you start by playing two rounds of trumps, you will have no protection against the heart suit. When the 4-1 trump break comes to light, the situation will be hopeless. Similarly, if you ruff a heart at trick two, you will not be able to duck a round of trumps and still have a trump left in dummy to guard against the defenders' hearts.

On the next deal you need to control exactly how many rounds of trumps are drawn. The best way to do this is to duck the first round of trumps, retaining the trump ace to prevent the defenders from drawing too many rounds of trumps.

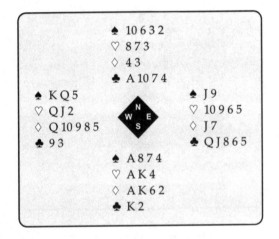

How will you play 4♠ when West leads the ♡Q?

You can afford to lose two trump tricks and one heart. Look at the losers in the South hand and you will see that you need to ruff both your diamond losers. What will happen if you attempt a diamond ruff before drawing any trumps at all? East will overruff from a doubleton trump. You will then lose two further trump tricks and one heart, going one down. Suppose instead that you start by playing ace and another trump. West can then beat you by drawing a third round of trumps, leaving dummy with only one trump with which to ruff two diamond losers.

The winning play is to duck a round of trumps at trick two. You can then win the defenders' return and draw a second round of trumps with your ace. Leaving a master trump at large, you cash two top diamonds, ruff a

diamond, return to your hand and ruff your last diamond. You will lose a heart and a second trump eventually, but the contract is yours.

Next we will see two deals where you duck a trump because your eventual intention is to 'draw trumps, ending in the dummy'. Few players would have seen the winning line here:

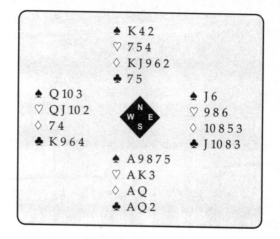

How will you play 6♠ when West leads the ♡Q?

Suppose you win the heart lead, unblock the ◇A-Q and continue with the ace and king of trumps. You will go down! When you start to run dummy's diamonds, West will ruff with his master trump and exit safely in hearts. Dummy's remaining trump pip is so small that you cannot use it as an entry.

You can avoid this problem by ducking a round of trumps at trick two. Let's say that East wins and returns the ♣J. You rise with the ♣A, play the two diamond honours in your hand and draw the remaining trumps with the ace and king. You can then cash dummy's three diamond winners, throwing a heart and two clubs from your hand.

We will end the Tip with a related deal where you not only have to duck a trump, you must duck it into the safe hand:

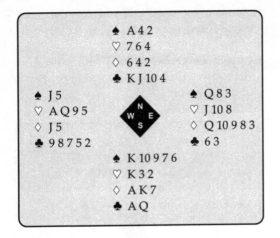

You reach 4♠ against silent opponents and West leads the ♣8. How will you play the contract?

Suppose you win with the ♣A, leaving yourself the option to overtake the ♣Q on the second round. You continue with a trump to the ace and a trump to the ten, ducking into the safe hand (West, who cannot attack hearts effectively). It's not good enough! West can play a second round of clubs and you will be in dummy for the last time with a trump still at large. East can ruff the next club and you will go two down.

You need to preserve the ace of trumps as an entry to dummy on the third round of the suit. The only way to make the contract is to win the first trick with dummy's ♣K, underplaying with your ♣Q. You then play a trump to the ten, ducking into the safe hand. Suppose that West plays another club, hoping his partner can ruff. You win with the bare ace and continue with the king and ace of trumps, 'drawing trumps, ending in the dummy'. You can then cash two more club tricks, throwing a heart and a diamond.

With the contract secure, you play a heart to the king, seeking an overtrick. The ♡A proves to be offside and you end with ten tricks. Are you disappointed to miss out on an overtrick? Not at all! With West holding the ♡A, your excellent early play was the only way to make the contract.

Tip

33

Think before finessing at trick one

B ridge has many 'wise sayings' and one of these is that many a contract is thrown away by careless play on the first trick. It's true! In this Tip we will see some deals where you will ditch a perfectly makeable contract if you are tempted to take a finesse at trick one.

One obvious situation is when you take an unnecessary risk that the opening lead is a singleton:

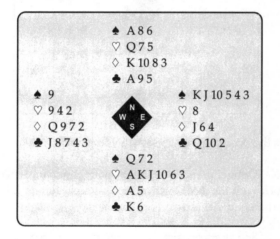

You arrive in 6♡ and West leads the ♠9. "Play low, partner." East wins with the ♠K and returns a spade, ruffed by West. The slam is one down and declarer shakes his head. "A 6-1 spade break!" he exclaims. "What are the odds against that?"

The first point to note is that most players lead a nine only when they have a doubleton or a singleton in the suit. (From 9-6-3 they would lead the 6 or the 3, according to their partnership's method.) So, when a nine is led there is quite a high chance that it is a singleton, even when there are seven cards missing in the suit.

The second point is this: when was the last time you saw someone lead a nine from a holding including the king? It's scarcely possible, is it? So, on this deal you should win the first trick with dummy's ♠A, draw

---

trumps and eventually lead towards the ♠Q. If you are the sort who likes to suck the last drop of juice from the orange, you can try to ruff down ◊Q-J-x from one of the defenders first.

The next deal is different. There is no significant risk of a ruff if you finesse on the first trick. However, your right-hand opponent will have the chance to make a damaging return in another suit.

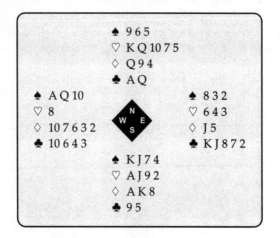

West leads the ♣3 against 4♡ How will you play?

It's a simple contract if you are familiar with elimination play. You win the first trick with the ♣A, draw trumps in three rounds and play three rounds of diamonds. These cards will remain:

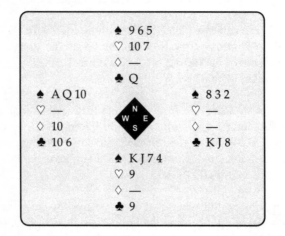

You exit in clubs, not caring which defender wins the trick. Here it will be East who wins. He cannot play another club, since this would give you a ruff-and-discard. So, he has to play a spade, you play low from your hand and West wins with the ♠10. West is now endplayed, forced to give you a trick with the ♠K or to concede a ruff-and-discard. The game is yours.

Do you see how the defenders can kill this play if you take an unwise club finesse at trick one? East will win with the king and switch to spades. West will win the trick with the lowest necessary card and exit safely with a club. There will then be no way to avoid the loss of two further spade tricks.

How could you tell that it was wrong to finesse the ♣Q at trick one? Only by making a plan for the contract before playing to the first trick (which in itself is one of the best Tips you will ever hear!)

Tip 34

Duck the opening lead into the safe hand

T he technique of ducking into the safe hand is a familiar one. An interesting variation can arise on the very first trick – when you have the ace facing a singleton in the suit that has been led.

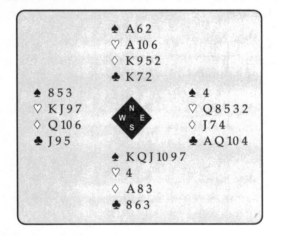

West leads the ♡7 against 4♠. How will you play?

You have four potential losers in the minors. One obvious chance is to find the ♣A onside. Another apparent possibility is that the diamonds break 3-3 and you can throw one of your club losers on the thirteenth diamond. To benefit from an even diamond break, you would have to duck a diamond into the safe (East) hand. If West were to gain the lead in diamonds, he could switch to the ♣J and the defenders would grab three club tricks before you had the chance of a discard.

Suppose you win the opening lead with dummy's ♡A, draw two rounds of trumps with the king and queen and lead the ◇3 towards dummy. You are hoping to play the ◇9, ducking the trick to East. All would be well if West held only one of the intermediate cards (◇Q, ◇J and ◇10). Even if he inserted this card on the first round, East would have to win the third round of diamonds. He could not attack clubs from his side of the table and you would eventually enjoy a discard. As the cards lie, though, West would insert the ◇10 on the first round and you could not set up a long diamond without the danger hand (West) gaining the lead.

To make the contract you must play the ♡10 at trick one! East (the safe hand) wins and cannot play clubs without giving you a trick. With diamonds 3-3, you are safe on any return. Suppose East returns another heart. You discard a diamond and draw two rounds of trumps with the king and queen. You then play the ◇A-K and ruff a third round of diamonds high in your hand. You can then cross to the ♠A, drawing West's last trump, and enjoy a club discard on the long diamond.

Another reason to duck the opening lead is because dummy's ace will be a valuable entry later in the play and you cannot afford it to be dislodged. That is the case here:

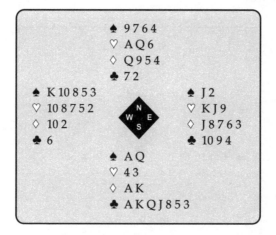

West leads the ♡5 against 6NT. How will you play the contract?

Suppose you finesse the ♡Q at trick one. If the finesse loses, East will return another heart, removing the entry to dummy. Unable to claim three diamond tricks, you will have to finesse in spades. You can guess what will happen there, with your luck! The finesse will fail and that will be one down.

Winning the first trick with the ♡A is no good, obviously. You would then have to bank everything on the spade finesse. No, the way to guarantee the contract is to play dummy's ♡6 on the first trick. East is welcome to win cheaply because he cannot damage you with his return. If he plays any suit but hearts, the ♡A will remain intact as an entry to untangle your diamond winners. If he does choose to return a heart, into dummy's tenace, you will have twelve tricks on top.

Defenders have an annoying habit of taking ruffs against you. It's a fact of life and when the cards lie in a certain way you have to accept it. Sometimes, though, you can reduce the damage by ensuring that the defenders do not ruff one of your precious honours. If they take their ruff, they will be ruffing a humble spot-card that was a loser anyway. Look at this typical deal, where many declarers would tumble to defeat:

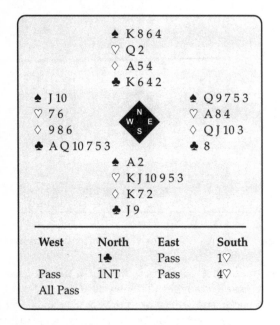

| ♠ K 8 6 4 |
| ♡ Q 2 |
| ◇ A 5 4 |
| ♣ K 6 4 2 |

♠ J 10	♠ Q 9 7 5 3
♡ 7 6	♡ A 8 4
◇ 9 8 6	◇ Q J 10 3
♣ A Q 10 7 5 3	♣ 8

| ♠ A 2 |
| ♡ K J 10 9 5 3 |
| ◇ K 7 2 |
| ♣ J 9 |

West	North	East	South
	1♣	Pass	1♡
Pass	1NT	Pass	4♡
All Pass			

West leads the ♠J and you win with the ace. When you play a trump to the queen, East wins with the ace and switches to the ♣8. West wins with the ♣A and returns the ♣Q. How will you play?

If you attempt to win the trick with dummy's ♣K you will go down. East will ruff, giving the defenders their third trick, and switch to the ◇Q. You will not then be able to avoid a subsequent loser in diamonds. To prevent the ♣K from being ruffed, you should play low from dummy on the second round of clubs. West's ♣Q wins the trick but you are safe on any continuation. If West plays another club, for example, you will withhold the ♣K again, ruff in the South hand and draw trumps. You can then cross to the ♠K to discard your diamond loser on the ♣K.

Sometimes your play to the first trick is affected by the risk of a subsequent ruff in the suit. Look at this deal:

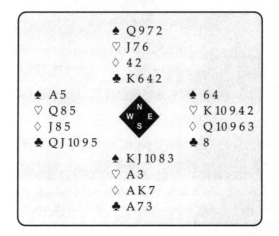

West leads the ♣Q against 4♠. You win with the ♣A and . . . Do you? In that case you are going down!

Let's see what happens if you fail to make a plan and win the first trick with the ♣A. When you play a trump, West will rise with the ♠A and continue with the ♣J. You cannot rescue the situation. Whether you play the ♣K immediately, or delay the moment for a trick or two, East will ruff the card into oblivion. You will end up one trick short.

You had no way of telling which defender would hold the ace of trumps. If anyone held a singleton in clubs, though, it was much more likely to be East than West. Players are not keen to lead a singleton queen, whereas a sequence headed by the Q-J-10 is attractive. You should guard against this situation by winning the first trick with dummy's ♣K. Now you will make the contract. West is welcome to win the first round of trumps and give his partner a club ruff. East will now be ruffing a loser. You will score four trump tricks, five side-suit winners and a diamond ruff in dummy.

Finally, here is a deal where you need to set up a long suit in the dummy. It is not practical to draw trumps first, so you must try to avoid a ruff as you set up the suit.

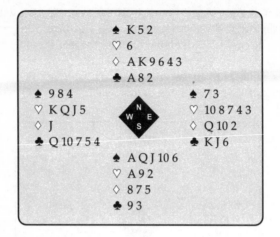

```
              ♠ K 5 2
              ♡ 6
              ◇ A K 9 6 4 3
              ♣ A 8 2

   ♠ 9 8 4                    ♠ 7 3
   ♡ K Q J 5      N           ♡ 10 8 7 4 3
   ◇ J         W     E        ◇ Q 10 2
   ♣ Q 10 7 5 4    S          ♣ K J 6

              ♠ A Q J 10 6
              ♡ A 9 2
              ◇ 8 7 5
              ♣ 9 3
```

West leads the ♡K against 6♠. How will you play the contract?

Suppose you win the heart lead and draw trumps in three rounds. All will be well if the defenders' diamonds split 2-2. If they break 3-1, though, you will have to surrender a diamond trick. You will be unprotected in hearts, when the defenders take their diamond winner, and will lose two tricks there.

An alternative line is to draw only two rounds of trumps, with the ace and queen, before playing the two top diamonds. You will then succeed when diamonds are 2-2 or the defender with a singleton diamond began with only two trumps and cannot ruff. In that case the ◇A-K will stand up and you can concede a third round of diamonds while there is a still a trump in dummy to protect you against a heart continuation.

Best of all is to combine this last line with leading towards dummy's diamond honours. West will not then be able to ruff a diamond honour even when he started with three trumps. You win the heart lead and draw one round of trumps with the ace. You then cross to the ◇A, return to the ♠Q and lead a second round of diamonds towards dummy. West cannot benefit by ruffing a loser, so he discards a heart. You win with dummy's ◇K and concede a diamond trick to East.

If East forces dummy to ruff a heart, you will return to your hand by ruffing a fourth round of diamonds. You can then draw the last trump and return to dummy with the ♣A. If instead East switches to a club, you will win with the ♣A, draw West's last trump with dummy's ♠K and claim the remaining tricks.

Ruff high
and then ruff low

Y ou have two cards to ruff in a suit and two trumps available in the dummy, one a low card and the other a master. Should you take the first ruff with the low trump or with the master trump? It depends on whether you can afford to lose a trick. If you cannot afford to lose a trick, you must take the first ruff with the low trump, risking an overruff. If the defenders cannot overruff, you are home. Your final ruff will be safe, with a master trump.

When you can afford to lose one trick but not two, it may be safer to take your first ruff with the master trump. It's difficult to visualise? Let's look at a typical deal:

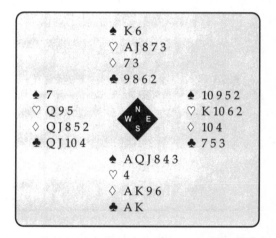

We will suppose first that you are in a contract of 7♠. West leads the ♣Q, sparing you a trump lead. How should you tackle the contract?

You need to ruff your two diamond losers. Since you cannot afford to lose a trick, you must take the first ruff with dummy's ♣6. If both defenders follow to this trick, you will return to your hand and ruff your last diamond with the ♣K. When you reach your hand again you will draw trumps, hoping that they break 3-2 and you have no loser there. With the cards lying as in the diagram you would go down, but there was no way to make the grand slam against that distribution.

Now let's suppose that you bid the hands less ambitiously and stop in the excellent contract of 6♠. Once more West leads the ♣Q. How will you play the contract now?

If you play the same way, ruffing the third round of diamonds with the ♠6, East will overruff and remove dummy's last trump. You will then go down in the small slam. To prevent this happening, you should ruff the third round of diamonds with the ♠K. East cannot overruff, of course, and you return to your hand to ruff your last diamond with the ♠6. Why do you do this, when you are almost certain that East can overruff? You take the ruff because if you draw trumps instead, and the trumps break 4-1, you will lose a trump trick and a diamond trick. Ruff the last diamond and you will lose just one trump trick, whether East decides to overruff or not.

The concept of ruffing high before ruffing low can sometimes show to advantage during a cross-ruff. Test yourself on this deal:

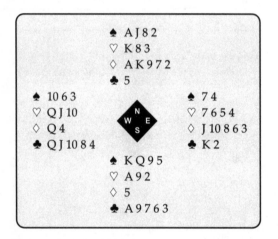

You reach 6♠ and West leads the ♡Q. How will you play?

You have five winners in the side suits. If you can score seven tricks in the trump suit, this will bring the total to twelve. You have excellent prospects of achieving this via a cross-ruff. You win the heart lead with the ace and play the two top diamonds, discarding a heart from your hand. You cash the ♡K and ruff a heart with the ♠5. You then play the ♣A and ruff a club with the ♠2. It was fairly safe to take these early ruffs with low trumps. In any case, the risk had to be taken. These cards are still to be played:

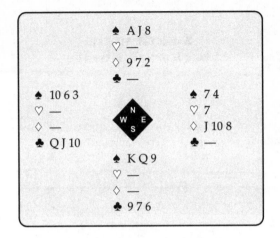

What now? If you were in a grand slam, you would need to score all six trumps separately. You would have no option but to ruff a diamond with the ♠9 and then ruff a club with the ♠8. If no overruff occurred, you could then score the remaining master trumps on a high cross-ruff. Playing in the small slam, you can afford to look for a safety play. It is not safe to ruff a diamond with the ♠9 because if West is out of diamonds, he may overruff with the ♠10 and return a trump, holding you to eleven tricks. Nor is it safe to ruff a club with dummy's ♠8. East might overruff and return a trump.

The safe line is to take the next four ruffs with master trumps, giving you the first eleven tricks. You will then have ♠9 in your hand and the ♠8 on the table. By leading another diamond, ruffing with the ♠9, you will be assured of the one further trump trick that you need.

What was the common factor in these two deals? It was right to ruff high (before ruffing low) because you could not afford a defender to overruff and return a trump.

D o you know what a 'backward finesse' is? You can use this
manoeuvre when you have a suit such as this:

Needing to score three spade tricks, you lead the ♠J from your hand. If
West plays low, perhaps thinking that you have ♠K-J-10 and are trying to
smoke out the queen, you allow the jack to run. If instead West covers
with the ♠Q, you win with the ♠A and finesse the ♠9 on the second
round. Again you score all three spade tricks.

How does this backward finesse compare with a straightforward finesse
of the ♠J? On most deals it is only half as good. A straightforward finesse
of the ♠J is a 50% prospect, winning whenever East holds the ♠Q. The
backward finesse is only a 25% chance, requiring two cards to be well
placed – West must hold the ♠Q and East must hold the ♠10.

You would not therefore use a backward finesse unless you were pretty
sure that West held the ♠Q and that a straightforward finesse of the ♠J
would fail. That is the case on this deal:

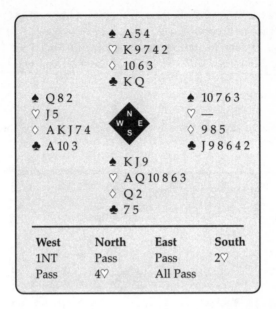

	♠ A 5 4		
	♡ K 9 7 4 2		
	◇ 10 6 3		
	♣ K Q		

♠ Q 8 2
♡ J 5
◇ A K J 7 4
♣ A 10 3

♠ 10 7 6 3
♡ —
◇ 9 8 5
♣ J 9 8 6 4 2

♠ K J 9
♡ A Q 10 8 6 3
◇ Q 2
♣ 7 5

West	North	East	South
1NT	Pass	Pass	2♡
Pass	4♡	All Pass	

West, whose 1NT showed 15-17 points, cashes the ◇A-K and the ♣A. How will you play when he continues with the ◇J, East following suit?

You ruff the third diamond and draw trumps in two rounds. What next? Many players would cross to the ♠A and finesse the ♠J at this stage but this is most unlikely to succeed. The defenders hold only 16 points between them and West's opening bid advertised 15-17 points. It follows that East can hold at most a jack in his hand. If he did not hold the ♠Q, West would be left with at most 14 points.

How can you score three spade tricks when West holds the ♠Q? One possibility is to drop the card doubleton. However, West began with only two hearts and it is unlikely that he opened 1NT with two doubletons in his hand. A better chance (you guessed it!) is to take a backward finesse. You lead the ♠J from your hand. If West plays low, you will run the jack successfully. If instead he covers with the ♠Q, you will win in the dummy and finesse the ♠9 on the way back. When the cards lie as in the diagram, you will make the contract.

We noted in the introductory text that a straightforward finesse of the jack was usually 50% and the backward finesse was 25%. What were the odds on this particular hand, given the information that West held 15-17 points? A straightforward finesse was a 0% prospect, because there was no room for East to hold the ♠Q. A backward finesse was at least 50% because you already knew that West held the ♠Q! Why 'at least' 50%, instead of exactly 50%? Well, the fact that West holds the ♠Q leaves him one less space to accommodate the ♠10. Let's suppose that West holds three or four spades, including the queen. In only fifteen out of the thirty-five possible holdings, will he also hold the ♠10. East will hold the ♠10 the remaining twenty times, giving the backward finesse a massive 57% chance of success!

We have space on this page for one more example of the backward finesse:

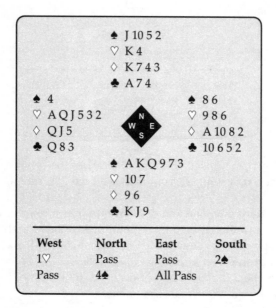

	♠ J 10 5 2	
	♡ K 4	
	◇ K 7 4 3	
	♣ A 7 4	
♠ 4		♠ 8 6
♡ A Q J 5 3 2		♡ 9 8 6
◇ Q J 5		◇ A 10 8 2
♣ Q 8 3		♣ 10 6 5 2
	♠ A K Q 9 7 3	
	♡ 10 7	
	◇ 9 6	
	♣ K J 9	

West	North	East	South
1♡	Pass	Pass	2♠
Pass	4♠	All Pass	

West leads the ◇Q against your game in spades. Since it is inconceivable that West holds the ◇A, you correctly play low from dummy. West cashes the ♡A at trick two and switches back to the ◇J, winning the third trick. When he plays the ◇5, you again play low from dummy and East produces the ◇10. How will you continue?

You ruff the third diamond and draw trumps in two rounds. A straight-forward finesse of the ♣J would give you the contract but can East holds the ♣Q? No, because he has already shown up with the ◇A and with 6 points he would surely have responded to the opening bid. As on the previous deal you will – yes, it's true – take a backward finesse. This will give you a 50% chance of making the game, whereas a normal finesse of the ♣J would be close to 0%. Not a difficult choice!

Tip
38

Use the dangerous entry first

S uppose you need to enter the dummy three times, perhaps to take three ruffs in your hand. Are there any situations when it is essential to use the entries in a particular order? Yes, indeed! Look at the next deal, for example:

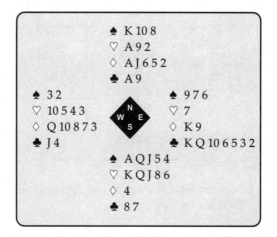

```
                    ♠ K 10 8
                    ♡ A 9 2
                    ◊ A J 6 5 2
                    ♣ A 9
  ♠ 3 2                          ♠ 9 7 6
  ♡ 10 5 4 3        N            ♡ 7
  ◊ Q 10 8 7 3   W     E         ◊ K 9
  ♣ J 4             S            ♣ K Q 10 6 5 3 2
                    ♠ A Q J 5 4
                    ♡ K Q J 8 6
                    ◊ 4
                    ♣ 8 7
```

You bid (brilliantly) to 7♠ and West leads the two of trumps. How will you play the contract?

You must aim to reverse the dummy, ruffing three diamonds in the South hand. This will give you three trump tricks, three diamond ruffs, two minor-suit aces and five heart tricks. The first trick is completed by the eight, nine and jack of trumps. You cross to dummy with the ◊A and ruff a diamond. Which entry should you use for the second diamond ruff – a trump, the ♡A or the ♣A?

There is only one right answer. The ♡A is a 'dangerous entry', because there is a risk that a defender will be able to discard hearts (as you ruff diamonds) and then be able to ruff the first round of hearts. The present Tip is that you should use the dangerous entry first. Here you must cross to the ♡A at trick four. The rest of the play will then cause no problem. You will ruff another diamond high, return to dummy with the ♣A, ruff a fourth diamond high and return to the ♠K to draw East's last trump.

If you use either of the other possible entries for the second diamond ruff, East will discard his singleton heart. With the heart entry to dummy a distant memory, the grand slam will go down. (Yes, as it happens, a heart or club lead would have given the grand slam no chance.)

Let's see one more example of this technique – a deal where the potential danger is perhaps more difficult to spot:

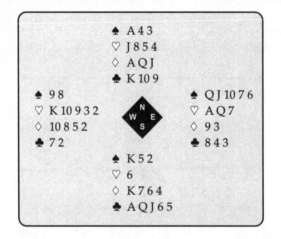

West leads the ♣2 against 6♣. Once again, you decide to play on reverse-dummy lines. How does the play go?

You win the trump lead with dummy's ♣9 and give up a heart. The defenders return a second round of trumps, won in the dummy, and you take your first heart ruff. At this stage it may not seem to matter whether you return to dummy with a spade or a diamond. Let's see what will happen, though, if you mistakenly cross to the ♠A.

You ruff another heart in the South hand and must now return to dummy with a diamond. When you ruff dummy's remaining heart, East will throw his last diamond! With no safe way to re-enter dummy to draw East's last trump, you will go down.

You have seven diamonds between the hands and only six spades. The 'dangerous entries' to dummy are therefore the two diamond entries. After taking the first heart ruff, you should use the first dangerous entry, crossing to the ◇A. You ruff a second heart and return to the second dangerous entry, the ◇Q. All is well when both defenders follow. You ruff dummy's last heart and return to dummy with the safe entry, the ♠A, to draw the last trump. The small slam is yours.

       52 Great Bridge Tips on Declarer Play

Tip
39

**Time your
ruffs correctly**

It may seem that little needs to be written about the technique of
ruffing losers in the dummy. Really? There are several quite tricky
situations that may arise. In this Tip we will look at those where you
have to prepare your ruffs before drawing trumps. We will start with a
relatively easy deal:

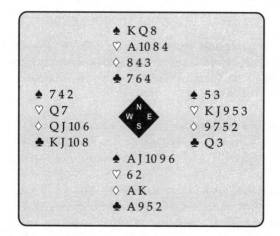

West leads the ◇Q against 4♠. What is your plan?

You have one loser in hearts and must avoid losing three further tricks in
the club suit. Since you have been spared a trump lead, you should be
able to ruff the fourth round of clubs in dummy (you will not need to if
the suit breaks 3-3, of course). You win the diamond lead and immediately
play ace and another club. If the defenders switch to a trump, you win
and concede another club. You can then win the trump return in the
South hand and ruff your last club. Returning to your hand with the
remaining diamond honour, you draw the last trump and claim the
contract. If you play even one round of trumps, before preparing for your
ruff, you will go down. The defenders will play a trump each time they
gain the lead in clubs.

Now let's look at something a little more difficult:

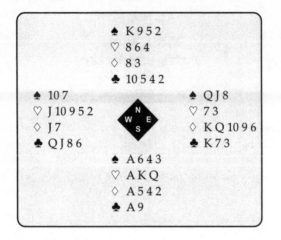

West leads the ♡J against 4♠. It looks easy enough. You will need a 3-2 trump break to restrict the trump losers to one. You can then afford to lose a club and a diamond, ruffing your other two diamond losers in the dummy. How will you play?

Suppose you win the heart lead and draw two rounds of trumps. When you give up a diamond to prepare for the ruff, the defenders can draw a third trump. Restricted to only one diamond ruff, you will go down.

Few players would make that mistake, it's true. Let's suppose instead that you draw just one round of trumps, with the ace, and then play ace and another diamond, preparing for your diamond ruffs. Not good enough! East can win the second round of diamonds and lead a third round, before you have had the chance to draw a second round of trumps. West will ruff with the ♠10 and you will then lose two trump tricks, whether or not you choose to overruff with dummy's ♠K. (The result would be the same if you had drawn the first round of trumps with dummy's king.)

The winning line of play is to draw just one round of trumps, in either hand, and then to *duck* a round of diamonds. The defenders can do you no damage. You will win their return and draw a second round of trumps. You can then ruff your two diamond losers at leisure, not minding when the defenders choose to take their trump trick.

Look back at the full deal. There were two traps to avoid. You had to prevent the defenders from drawing a third round of trumps. You also had to prevent a trump promotion when you conceded a diamond trick. It was a more difficult deal than it looked!

When you are planning to take ruffs in both hands – the familiar cross-ruff – it can be essential to cash your winners in the side suits before you start ruffing, otherwise the defenders may have a chance to discard and eventually ruff one of your side-suit winners. Only a strong player would make the following contract:

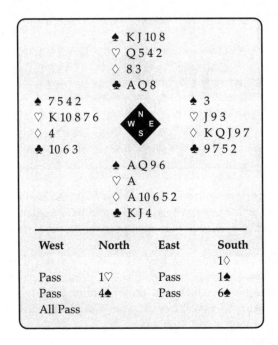

	♠ K J 10 8		
	♡ Q 5 4 2		
	◇ 8 3		
	♣ A Q 8		

♠ 7 5 4 2		♠ 3
♡ K 10 8 7 6		♡ J 9 3
◇ 4		◇ K Q J 9 7
♣ 10 6 3		♣ 9 7 5 2

	♠ A Q 9 6	
	♡ A	
	◇ A 10 6 5 2	
	♣ K J 4	

West	North	East	South
			1◇
Pass	1♡	Pass	1♠
Pass	4♠	Pass	6♠
All Pass			

A trump lead would have worked well, as it happens, but West leads the ◇4. You have five potential winners in the side suits. If you can add one trump trick and six ruffing tricks, this will bring the total to twelve. You win the diamond lead with the ace. What now?

The answer is that you had better cash your three club tricks. If instead you concede a diamond, preparing for the ruff, West will throw one of his clubs. You will not then be able to score the three club tricks that you need. There is no point worrying that one of the clubs may be ruffed. Unless clubs break 4-3, you have little chance of making the contract. (You can guess from West's lead into your bid diamond suit that he has a singleton and there is no chance of setting up the diamonds.)

You cash three club winners and the defenders follow all the way. You then concede a diamond trick, preparing for the cross-ruff. Whatever East chooses to return, you will score the seven trump tricks that you need.

We will end the Tip with a somewhat exotic hand on the same theme:

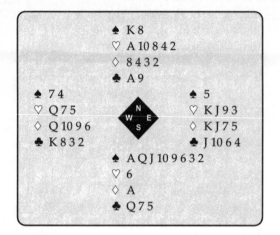

You reach a small slam in spades and West finds the aggravating lead of the ♣4. If he had led any other suit, you could have made the slam easily by ruffing a club. How will you attempt to recover the situation?

East produces the ♠5 on the first trick. Who do you think holds the missing trump? The odds are high that it is West. Players hate to lead a singleton trump in case this picks up an honour in partner's hand. It is much more likely that West has led from a doubleton trump. How can you take advantage of this inference?

One possible line of play is to draw trumps, play a club to the ace and lead towards the ♣Q. If East holds the ♣K you will make the slam. A better idea is to try to duck a club to East, the safe hand who cannot remove dummy's last trump. You win the first trick in the South hand and lead the ♣5, playing the ♣9 from dummy. East has to win the trick and, as you predicted, has no trump to return. You win the diamond return with the ace and soon arrange a club ruff in dummy. The slam is yours.

If West had held ♣K-10-3-2 he could insert the ♣10 on the first round. You would win with the ace and return the ♣9. If East covered with the ♣J, you would have the option of ducking in your hand! Again East would not be able to return a trump.

When an honour falls, assume that it was bare

Time after time, you will encounter some card combination where an honour falls from one of the defenders and you have to judge whether the honour was bare or part of an honour combination. Many players go through their entire bridge careers without understanding how the odds lie in such situations. It is a difficult area and we will cover it in this Tip. Look at this everyday situation:

♠ A 10 6 4 3

♠ K 8 7 2

You cash the king on the first round and the queen or jack appears from East. Should you finesse the ♠10 on the next round or play to the ace, hoping that East started with queen-jack doubleton?

If you have not read about this situation before, you may be surprised to hear that the odds are around 2-to-1 in favour of East's honour being a singleton. The easiest way to understand this is by realising that the three combinations Q-J doubleton, Q singleton and J singleton are all equally likely (in rough terms). So, whenever one of the honours falls it is twice as likely to be a singleton as to be a chosen card from the doubleton. Suppose the situation arose thirty times. These would be divided as follows:

East holds ♠Q-J	10 times
East holds ♠Q	10 times
East holds ♠J	10 times

If you always finesse the ♠10 on the second round, whichever honour appears from East on the first round, you will pick up the suit twenty times out of thirty. You will achieve this happy rate of success regardless of East's chosen strategy when he is dealt Q-J doubleton. (It makes absolutely no difference whether this particular East always plays the queen from Q-J, always plays the jack or chooses a card at random. Following the recommended line, you will lose a trick to Q-J anyway.)

Every time you discuss this type of situation with a group of bridge players, at least one of them will not believe these 2-to-1 odds. He will say: "When the queen shows, you can forget about the ten cases for the singleton jack. You are only comparing the ten cases for Q-J doubleton with the ten cases for singleton queen."

Do you see why this argument is fallacious? You cannot place all ten cases for Q-J doubleton into the scales because half the time (on average), the defender would have chosen to play the jack from this combination. So, on average, you should be comparing five cases of Q-J doubleton with ten cases of queen singleton, again giving you 2-to-1 odds.

It is because of the fallacy just described that so many players do not accept (in truth, they simply don't understand) why you get 2-to-1 odds by playing for the honour to be singleton. Rest assured that the world's mathematicians and statisticians do understand the situation and are on our side! Discuss it with some university Mathematics lecturer and he will nod his head learnedly. "It's an application of Bayes' Theorem, isn't it?" The odds are indeed 2-to-1 in your favour, as you will discover if you start following this recommendation at the bridge table.

The technical name for the idea, in a bridge context, is the Principle of Restricted Choice. Let's see some more examples of how you can use it as an aid to choosing the best line of play.

This is a common position:

You finesse the ◊J on the first round, losing to the queen or king. When you regain the lead, you play a second round of the suit towards dummy. West follows with an unhelpful spot card. What should you do?

There are three holdings for East where this situation will arise: ◊K-Q doubleton, ◊K singleton and ◊Q singleton. If you finesse again on the second round, the recommended play, you will win two times out of three. The odds are 2-to-1 in your favour.

This situation is similar:

♡ K 9 6 5

♡ A Q 4

You cash the ace and queen and on the second round the jack or ten appears from East. This will happen whenever East started with ♡J-10-x, ♡J-x or ♡10-x. These three holdings are roughly equal in probability, so finessing the ♡9 on the third round will give you odds of 2-to-1 in your favour.

Move all the cards down by one pip (always an interesting thing to do) and a similar situation arises:

♡ Q 8 5 4

♡ K J 3

You lead low to the king and West wins with the ace. When you regain the lead and cash the jack, the 10 or 9 appears from East. This will happen when East has one of these holdings: ♡10-9-x, ♡10-x and ♡9-x. Finesse the ♡8 on the third round and the odds (you will not be surprised to hear) will be 2-to-1 in your favour.

The situation is the same if we move the cards down one more notch:

♡ J 7 4 3

♡ Q 10 2

Your best chance here is to lead twice towards the South hand. Much of the time you will easily score the two tricks you seek (when East started with A-x or K-x, for example, his honour will appear on the second round). Let's suppose that the queen loses to West's king and, on the second round, the ten loses to West's ace. Meanwhile, the ♡8 or ♡9 falls from East on the second round. When you lead towards dummy's ♡J-7 on the third round, a low spot card appears from West. Should you finesse or not?

Exactly the same logic applies. The situation will arise whenever East began with ♡9-8-x, ♡9-x or ♡8-x. By finessing the ♡7 on the third round, you will succeed when East began with one of the doubleton combinations. The odds are 2-to-1 in your favour.

The odds are even more strikingly in your favour when three touching honours are missing:

You cash the king and queen and East follows with one of these pairs: ♣J-10, ♣J-9 or ♣10-9. When you lead the ♣2 towards dummy's ♣A-8 on the third round, West produces the last low spot card. Will you finesse the ♣8 or play for the drop?

The four combinations: ♣J-10-9, ♣J-10, ♣J-9 and ♣10-9 are roughly equal in probability. Whichever two of these cards fall from East on the first two rounds, the odds are 3-to-1 that they were forced cards from a doubleton rather than chosen cards from ♣J-10-9. You should therefore finesse the ♣8 on the third round.

Let's round off the Tip with a full deal:

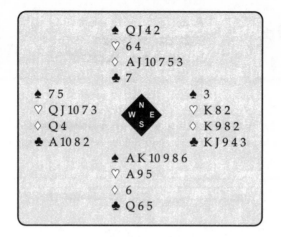

How will you play 6♠ when West leads the ♡Q?

You win with the ♡A and draw one round of trumps with the ace. You must now attempt to set up dummy's diamond suit. You cross to the ◇A and ruff a low diamond, the queen falling from West. You return to dummy with a trump honour and lead the ◇J, East following low. Should you run the ◇J (playing East for the missing ◇K), or should you ruff (playing West for the ◇K)?

Surprise, surprise, it is an example of Restricted Choice. The three holdings for West: ◇K-Q-x, ◇K-x and ◇Q-x are all roughly equal in probability. So, when the king or queen appears from West on the second round, you will get odds of 2-to-1 in your favour by running the ◇J next. Justice is done on the present deal when the ruffing finesse succeeds and you make your ambitious slam.

Many of the recommended plays in this book of Tips will give you only a small percentage in your favour. The Principle of Restricted Choice is different. It offers you a massive edge! Two-to-one odds, at least. You simply cannot afford to ignore it or to be one of those doubters who allow themselves to be swayed by the fallacy that we looked at a page or two ago. Such poor souls go through their lives with the two-to-one odds stacked against them!

Tip 41

Bad players lead from jacks

Sometimes you are faced with a critical guess at trick one. West has led a low card from an honour. Does he hold the king or the jack?

♠ Q 9 2
♡ K Q 10 6
◇ Q 10 7
♣ A K 5

◇2 led

♠ A K J 10 8 3
♡ 4
◇ A 5
♣ Q J 4 2

West leads the ◇2 against 6♠. Do you play the ◇Q or the ◇10?'

If either defender holds both missing diamond honours, your play will make no difference. So, the only interesting cases are when West has led from J-x-x-x or K-x-x-x. Which is more likely?

The answer may surprise you. Poor players are terrified of leading from a king and very rarely do it. If you are playing at your local club, against someone who usually finishes in the lower half of the ranking list, the odds are high that he is leading from the ◇J. You should insert dummy's ◇10, hoping that this will force the ◇K from East.

Now suppose that West is an expert. Such players hate leading from a jack! Leading from a king, however, is a different matter. Particularly against a suit slam, such a lead may well strike gold. Partner may hold the queen and a second trick can be set up – to go with a certain winner, such as an ace or a sure trump trick. So, when you have a high regard for the player in the West seat, rise with dummy's queen!

Tip 42

Concede a trump trick to gain an entry

When reaching dummy may be worth two tricks, it can be worthwhile to sacrifice one trick to establish an entry. In this Tip we will see some of the ways in which this can be done in the trump suit. Look at this deal, for example:

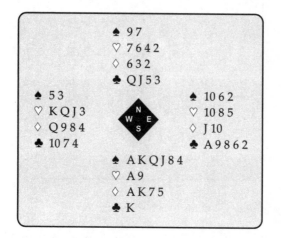

You bid to 4♠ and West leads the ♡K. How will you play the contract?

You win the heart lead with the ace. If your next move is to draw trumps, you are unlikely to make the contract unless diamonds break 3-3. A slightly better line is to play ace, king and another diamond, planning to ruff the fourth round of diamonds with dummy's ♠9. Here East holds the ♠10, though, and will defeat you by overruffing. What else can you try?

By far the best line is to lead the ♣K at trick two. If East holds up the ♣A you will make the contract easily, losing just three tricks in the red suits. Let's suppose that East captures the first round of clubs and cashes the ♡10. He then switches to the ◇J, which you win. What now?

Two club winners await you in the dummy and you can fight your way there in the trump suit. Your next move is to lead the ♠4 to dummy's ♠7. East wins with the ♠10 and plays another diamond. You win with the ◇K and cross to dummy with the ♠9. You then throw two losers on the ♣Q-J,

---

return to the South hand with a high ruff and draw the last trump. Game made! If West is a rival of yours, you can point out to him that a trump lead would have beaten the contract. It would remove prematurely the potential entry to dummy.

On the next deal you may well have a trump loser anyway. By offering a definite trump trick to the defenders, you set up an entry to dummy (or avoid the potential trump loser).

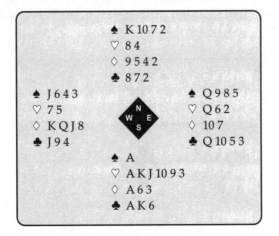

How will you play 4♡ when West leads the ◇K?

There is no entry to dummy for a trump finesse but you have some chance of escaping a trump loser by laying down the ace and king. If the ♡Q does not drop in two rounds you are almost certain to go down, losing three subsequent tricks in the minor suits. What else can you try?

You should win the diamond lead and cash the ♠A. Next you lead the ♡J from your hand. East now has two losing alternatives. If he refuses to win with the ♡Q, you will score six trump tricks to go with your four winners in the side suits. If instead East wins with the ♡Q, he will set up dummy's ♡8 as an entry. You will be able to cross to dummy and throw your club loser on the ♠K.

Dummy held only one side-suit winner on that deal but it was still profitable to surrender a trump trick to reach it. That's because you were likely to have a trump loser anyway. You would play the same way with ♡A-K-Q-10-9-3. Since you might lose a trump trick to ♡J-x-x-x, you would unblock the ♠A and lead the ♡10 from your hand.

We will end the Tip with a deal where the reward for reaching dummy will be the chance to take a finesse:

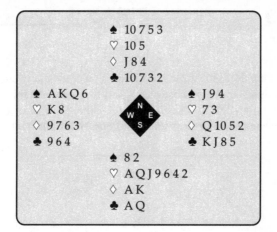

```
              ♠ 10 7 5 3
              ♡ 10 5
              ◇ J 8 4
              ♣ 10 7 3 2
♠ A K Q 6                      ♠ J 9 4
♡ K 8          N               ♡ 7 3
◇ 9 7 6 3    W   E             ◇ Q 10 5 2
♣ 9 6 4        S               ♣ K J 8 5
              ♠ 8 2
              ♡ A Q J 9 6 4 2
              ◇ A K
              ♣ A Q
```

West leads the ♠K against 4♡. He continues with the ♠A, his partner playing upwards to show three cards in the suit. At trick three West continues with a low spade to East's jack. How will play the contract?

You ruff the third round of spades and see that you have potential further losers in both trumps and clubs. If your next move is to cash the ace of trumps, you will almost certainly go down unless the ♡K falls. A better chance is to attempt to reach dummy with the ♡10, so that you can take a club finesse.

There are two possible lines of play. One is to lead the ♡Q from your hand. If a defender wins with the ♡K, you can cross to dummy's ♡10 on the second round. This line will fail if a defender holds three or more trumps to the king and is smart enough to hold up the king. The other possibility is to lead low towards dummy's ♡10, hoping that the ♡K is onside. Which is better, do you think?

Leading towards the ♡10 gives you a 50% chance of reaching dummy (and therefore a 25% chance of making the contract, since you will also need the club finesse to be right). The alternative line of leading the ♡Q will allow you to reach dummy – or pick up the trumps without loss – when hearts are 2-2 or the ♡K is singleton, which is a total of 53%. So, leading the ♡Q is slightly better. Also, some defenders might mistakenly win from ♡K-x-x. Whichever of these lines you adopt, you will be giving yourself a hugely better chance than if you simply lay down the ace of trumps.

Tip 43

Avoid a blockage in the trump suit

Allowing a suit to become blocked is one of the many embarrassing situations that may arise during a bridge game. In this Tip we will look at a slightly unusual topic – some ways in which you can avoid a blockage in the trump suit. Test yourself on this deal:

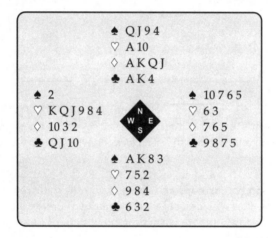

West, who opened with a weak two-bid in hearts leads the ♡K against your small slam in spades. How will you play the contract?

Dummy's fourth diamond will take care of your club loser, so one heart ruff in dummy will bring the total to twelve. You draw one round of trumps, with dummy's queen, and then concede a round of hearts. West wins and switches to the ♣Q. What now?

You need to cross to your hand, ruff a heart and then return to your hand to draw trumps. To achieve this, you should lead the ♠9 to your ♠A. You unblock the ♠9 so that you can later lead the ♠4 towards your ♠K-8, should West show out on the second round of trumps. West does indeed show out. You ruff your last heart with dummy's ♠J and lead the carefully preserved ♠4 for a finesse of the ♠8. You can then draw East's last trump with the ace and claim the contract.

Do you see what will go wrong if you do not unblock the ♠9, by leading it on the second round? When you ruff the third round of hearts with the ♠J, East will discard one of his diamonds. You will be left with the ♠9 in dummy opposite the ♠K-8 in your hand. East will not cover the ♠9 and you will then be stuck in dummy. When you continue with three rounds of diamonds, East will beat the slam by ruffing the third round.

On the deal we have just seen, you were forced to take the heart ruff with a high trump in order to avoid an overruff. On the next deal you must ruff with a higher trump than is necessary, purely to avoid a blockage:

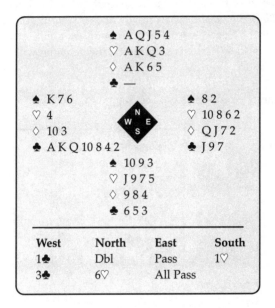

West	North	East	South
1♣	Dbl	Pass	1♡
3♣	6♡	All Pass	

So far as you can recall, it is the weakest hand on which you have ever ended as declarer in a slam. West leads the ♣A. How will you play?

Your eventual intention is to lead spades from the South hand. To create a trump entry to your hand, you should ruff the opening club lead with dummy's ♡A. When you continue with the king and queen of trumps, West shows out on the second round. This causes no problem after your previous unblock. You lead the ♡3 to your ♡9 and draw East's trump with the ♡J. Finally you run the ♠10, breathing freely again when the finesse wins. Five spade tricks and the slam are yours.

What would happen if you ruffed the first trick with the ♡3? You might survive if trumps broke 3-2. (After just two rounds of trumps you could reach your hand for a spade finesse by ruffing the fourth diamond.) With the cards lying as in the diagram, you would go down.

Whenever you lead towards dummy, it is relatively easy for the defender in the second seat to make the correct play. That's because he can see the cards that are sitting over him, in the dummy. Life in the second seat is nowhere near so comfortable when you lead towards the closed hand. Providing you are holding your cards up (which is a first-rate Tip in its own right!), the defender will often have to guess what to do.

Many declarers would miss the best play on this deal:

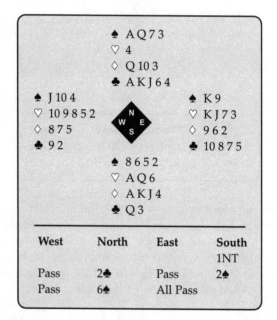

West	North	East	South
			1NT
Pass	2♣	Pass	2♠
Pass	6♠	All Pass	

With only ♠8-6-5-2 in your hand, you are alarmed when partner leaps to a small slam in the suit. (Indeed, some players would have responded 2◇ to Stayman, denying a four-card major.) How will you play the slam when West leads the ♡10?

Most declarers would take a simple view of the deal. They would win the heart lead with the queen and lead a trump to dummy's queen. When the finesse lost to East's king the slam would be one down. "I don't think much of your spade suit," North would observe.

You can give yourself a better chance by crossing to the ♦10 at trick two and leading the ♠3 from dummy. What should East do when he holds ♠K-x? Many defenders would go in with the king. With only one trick to be lost in the trump suit, you would then make the slam.

It is not correct defence for East to rise with the king from ♠K-x, of course. If you held the ♠J, you would hardly lead the suit from dummy. You would lead low to the ♠Q, hoping to find a doubleton king onside. So, East should play low smoothly, expecting his partner to win the first round of trumps. You would then have no reason to spurn a finesse of the queen on the second round of spades.

In practice, it makes little difference to you as declarer what East should or should not do if he holds ♠K-x. All that concerns you is that there are many, many defenders out there who will go wrong and put up the ♠K. Take advantage of it! Leading a low trump from dummy on the first round may make the difference between picking up the slam bonus and going one down.

This particular play (low from A-Q-x-x opposite x-x-x-x) has an even greater chance of succeeding when the suit involved is a side suit. It is then more plausible that you might be leading from A-Q-x-x towards J-x or a singleton jack in the closed hand.

Let's see another deal where you can give East a tough time:

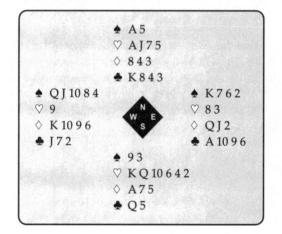

West leads the ♠Q against 4♡. How will you play the contract?

You have four potential losers awaiting you. There is one technical chance of making the contract. Suppose East holds ♣A-x-x (or ♣A-x). After winning the spade lead, you can lead towards the ♣Q. If the queen wins, you will draw trumps in two rounds and duck a second round of clubs. You can then win the diamond return, cross to dummy with a trump and ruff a club. When East began with ♣A-x-x his ace will appear on the third round and you can return to dummy with another trump to discard a diamond loser on the established ♣K.

Look at the diagram and you will see that East does not have such a helpful club holding. Nevertheless, he will have some difficult decisions to make if you play the hand properly. Win the first trick with the ♠A and lead a low club from the table. What should East do on this trick? If you have a singleton ♣Q, he will do best to rise with the ♣A. He can then cash a spade and switch to the ◇Q, beating the contract when his partner holds the ◇A. Since you have applied pressure by playing a club immediately, many Easts would suspect a singleton ♣Q in the South hand and give away the contract by rising with the ace. You would then have two club tricks and could discard one of your diamond losers.

Let's suppose that this East is a cool customer. He thinks for a few moments and then plays the ♣6. You win the trick with the ♣Q. What now? You should cross to dummy with the ♡A and lead another low club towards your hand! Again this will apply pressure on East. His partner's ♣2 on the first round (a count signal) will have told him that you have one club left. If this is the jack, his best defence is to rise with the ♣A and cash the ♠K. He would then switch to the ◇Q, hoping for two tricks in that suit.

Let's suppose that this East is a *very* cool customer. After considering the matter for quite a time, he plays the ♣9 on the second round and wins the trick with it. He switches to the ◇Q and when you subsequently fail to ruff out the ♣A you will go one down. Don't worry about it. You did every thing you could! Against a lesser opponent in the East seat your pressure play would have succeeded.

Tip
45

Use your imagination to gain an entry

Y ou need to reach the dummy, so you lead a low spade and win with dummy's ♠A. Effective, yes, but hardly worthy of applause from the kibitzers. In this Tip we will look at some more imaginative and spectacular ways in which you may be able to fight your way to the table. Test yourself on this deal:

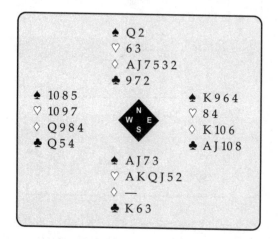

You arrive in 4♡ and West leads the ♡10, which you win with the ♡A. How will you play the deal?

Suppose your next move is a spade to dummy's queen. All will be well if West holds the ♠K. If he rises with the card, you will have three spade tricks and an entry to dummy. You will make at least ten tricks. When East holds the ♠K, the situation will be far less bright. He will win and return another trump, to prevent a spade ruff. You can draw trumps and exit on the fourth round of spades, forcing the defenders to play a club for you, but you will still lose two spades and two clubs. What else can you try?

At trick two you should lead the ♠J from your hand. As the cards lie, the defenders can do nothing. If East wins with the ♠K and returns a trump, you will win in your hand and draw the last trump. You can then cross to the ♠Q and discard a loser on the ◇A. Finally you will lead towards

---

the ♣K for the contract. East cannot afford to duck the ♠J because you would then cash the ♠A, ruff a spade and end with an overtrick.

On the next deal you arrive in what is possibly not the best contract:

```
                    ♠ 8 6
                    ♡ A K 9 5 3 2
                    ◊ 10 9 3
                    ♣ 5 3
  ♠ Q 10 7 2                        ♠ J 9 5 3
  ♡ 10 8 4           N              ♡ Q J 7 6
  ◊ J 4          W       E          ◊ Q 8 7
  ♣ Q 10 8 2         S              ♣ J 9
                    ♠ A K 4
                    ♡ —
                    ◊ A K 6 5 2
                    ♣ A K 7 6 4
```

West	North	East	South
			1◊
Pass	1♡	Pass	3♣
Pass	3♡	Pass	3NT
All Pass			

A contract of 6◊ would have succeeded, as the cards lie. (East can over-ruff the third club but this absorbs his natural trump trick.) Partner will be less impressed by your complaints about his bidding if you put 3NT on the floor. How will you play when West leads the ♣2?

You have six top tricks and, unless one of the defenders holds ◊Q-J-x-x, can establish two more by playing ace and another diamond. The defenders will then clear the spades, however, and you will not have time to set up a ninth trick unless clubs are 3-3. Is there anything better?

You must cut your way through to dummy and the two precious jewels sitting there in the heart suit. Win the first trick and lead a low diamond towards dummy. You are hoping that West will hold at least one of the missing honours and that you can set up a dummy entry in the suit. Suppose West wins with the ◊J and clears the spade suit. You then lead another low diamond, dummy's ◊10 forcing East's queen. The defenders can now score a total of two spades and two diamonds but the ◊9 will provide an entry to dummy's two heart winners and nine tricks are yours.

Hold up an
ace even in
a suit contract

Holding up an ace is a familiar procedure when playing in a no-
trump contract. The purpose is to exhaust one defender of his
cards in the suit. If he gains the lead subsequently, the commu-
nication to his partner's hand will be broken. Less familiar perhaps is the
use of the same tactic in a suit contract. The purpose is the same, though.
By exhausting one opponent of his cards in the suit led, you prevent the
defenders from cashing their full quota of winners. We will start with a
straightforward example:

	♠ 9 8 5 3	
	♡ A 2	
	◇ A 7 6 4	
	♣ A J 3	
♠ 7		♠ A 4
♡ Q 9 8 5 3		♡ J 10 7 4
◇ Q J 10 8		◇ K 2
♣ 7 5 4		♣ K 10 9 6 2
	♠ K Q J 10 6 2	
	♡ K 6	
	◇ 9 5 3	
	♣ Q 8	

West	North	East	South
	1◇	Pass	1♠
Pass	2♠	Pass	4♠
All Pass			

How should you play the contract when West leads the ◇Q?

Let's see first what will happen if you win the first trick with dummy's
ace. If East is a competent performer, he will unblock his ◇K. When you
play a trump, East will win with the ♠A and the defenders will cash two
winners in diamonds. You will have to take the club finesse and will be
one down when that fails.

Let's start again and hold up dummy's ◊A at trick one, aiming to exhaust East of his cards in diamonds. East can do no better than to overtake with the ◊K and return the suit, West's ◊8 driving out dummy's ace. You cross to the ♡K and run the ♣Q to East. The finesse loses but, thanks to your hold up, East has no diamond to play. He could cross in trumps if West held the ♠A but fortune is with you and East holds that card. Whatever the defenders do from this point, you will be able to discard your diamond loser on the third round of clubs. The contract is yours.

On the next deal you must combine a hold-up with a subsequent avoidance play, to keep the danger hand off lead.

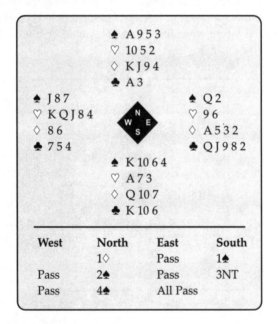

West	North	East	South
	1◊	Pass	1♠
Pass	2♠	Pass	3NT
Pass	4♠	All Pass	

West leads the ♡K against your spade game, East playing the ♡9. How will you play the contract?

You should hold up your ace on the first round of hearts, hoping that the suit divides 5-2 and you can break the communications between the defenders. Even if West happens to hold six hearts he can do you little damage. If East were to ruff the second round of hearts, he would be ruffing a loser and perhaps exhausting a natural trump trick.

As it happens, East follows with the ♡6 on the second round of hearts. You win with the ♡A and must consider your play in trumps. Suppose you play the ace and king of trumps, both defenders following. When you play on diamonds, East (the safe hand) will win and has no heart to play, thanks to your hold up at trick one. When you regain the lead and revert to diamonds, your luck will change. West will ruff the third round with his master trump and cash the setting trick in hearts.

To make the contract, you must cash the ♠K and then finesse the ♠9 into the safe hand. You can then win East's return, draw the last trump and establish the diamonds, eventually enjoying a discard on dummy's fourth diamond.

On the next deal you hold up an ace for a different reason. You want to keep the danger hand off lead.

```
              ♠ K Q 5
              ♡ K 8 2
              ◇ J 7 4
              ♣ A 10 7 3
♠ 2                          ♠ 8 7 4
♡ J 9 7 5        N           ♡ A Q 4 3
◇ Q 9 8 2      W   E         ◇ K 10 6 5
♣ 9 8 4 2        S           ♣ K 6
              ♠ A J 10 9 6 3
              ♡ 10 6
              ◇ A 3
              ♣ Q J 5
```

West	North	East	South
			1♠
Pass	2♣	Pass	2♠
Pass	4♠	All Pass	

West leads the ◇2 against your spade game. You play low from dummy and East correctly inserts the ◇10. How will you play?

Let's see what will happen if you forget that you are in the middle of reading a Tip on 'holding up aces'. You win the first trick with the ◇A, draw trumps in three rounds and run the ♣Q. East wins with the ♣K and sees that he needs to put West on lead to play a heart through dummy's king. He returns the ◇5, underleading his king, and West wins with the ◇Q. A heart switch then defeats you.

Let's go back to trick one and test out the current Tip. You hold up the

◊A, allowing East's ◊10 to win. Why do you do that? Because you want to prevent West – the danger hand who can play a heart through dummy's ♡K – from gaining the lead. The defenders cannot beat you now. You win the diamond return, draw trumps and run the ♣Q. East wins with the ♣K but has no way to reach his partner's hand. He will doubtless play the ◊K. You ruff and play three more rounds of clubs, discarding one of your hearts. The contract is yours.

Finally we will see a deal where you hold up an ace in order to avoid an enemy ruff. The contract was originally misplayed in an international match between New Zealand and Morocco. See if you would have done better.

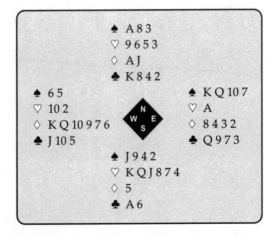

You arrive in 4♡ and West leads the ♣6. How will you play the contract?

The original declarer gave the matter insufficient thought. He rose with dummy's ♣A and led a trump. East won with the bare ♡A and cashed the ♠K-Q. When he played a fourth round of spades, South had to follow suit and West was able to ruff with the ♡10. One down!

The safe way to play the hand is to play low from dummy on the first trick. East wins with the ♣Q and cannot damage you even if the opening lead was a singleton. At worst, if the ♣6 was a singleton, West would ruff one of your losing spades. You would lose a subsequent trick to the ace of trumps but that is all. Ten tricks would be yours.

Tip

47

**Lead through the
trump ace to avoid
a promotion**

It is a familiar avoidance play technique to lead through a defender's ace. If he rises with the ace in the second seat, capturing nothing with it, this may give you an extra trick. If instead he ducks, you will gain a tempo – perhaps scoring a trick in that suit and then switching to a different suit. This Tip explores an unusual form of such a play, where the defender's ace is the ace of trumps.

Would you have seen the danger on the following deal?

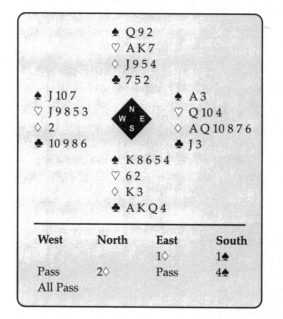

	♠ Q 9 2	
	♡ A K 7	
	◇ J 9 5 4	
	♣ 7 5 2	
♠ J 10 7		♠ A 3
♡ J 9 8 5 3		♡ Q 10 4
◇ 2		◇ A Q 10 8 7 6
♣ 10 9 8 6		♣ J 3
	♠ K 8 6 5 4	
	♡ 6 2	
	◇ K 3	
	♣ A K Q 4	

West	North	East	South
		1◇	1♠
Pass	2◇	Pass	4♠
All Pass			

North's cue-bid shows a sound raise to at least 2♠. Since your hand is close to a maximum for a one-level overcall, you leap to 4♠. West leads the ◇2 to his partner's ace and ruffs the diamond return with the ♠7. He then switches to the ♣10. How will you play from this point?

There are only 15 points out, so East (who opened the bidding) is a big favourite to hold the ♠A. Suppose you win the club switch and lead a trump to the queen. East will win with the ace and return another diamond.

This will promote West's bare ♠J, which lies behind your ♠K.

To avoid this unpleasant demise of your contract, you should lead the first round of trumps from dummy. You win the club switch, cross to the ♡A and lead a low trump. East now has two losing alternatives. If he rises with the ♠A, you will be left with the king and queen of trumps. You can ruff his diamond continuation with the ♠K and draw the two outstanding trumps with dummy's ♠Q. A trump will remain in dummy to ruff the fourth round of clubs.

Suppose instead that East plays low on the first round of trumps. You will win with the king and play a second round, drawing all the enemy trumps. You can see what a difference it makes to lead the first round of trumps through the defenders' ace.

Here is another deal where the defenders threaten a trump promotion:

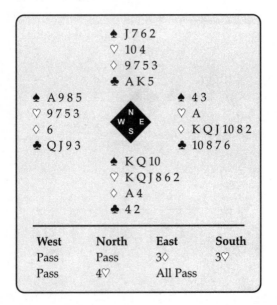

	♠ J 7 6 2	
	♡ 10 4	
	◊ 9 7 5 3	
	♣ A K 5	
♠ A 9 8 5		♠ 4 3
♡ 9 7 5 3		♡ A
◊ 6		◊ K Q J 10 8 2
♣ Q J 9 3		♣ 10 8 7 6
	♠ K Q 10	
	♡ K Q J 8 6 2	
	◊ A 4	
	♣ 4 2	

West	North	East	South
Pass	Pass	3◊	3♡
Pass	4♡	All Pass	

East opens with a typical third-seat pre-empt and, sitting South, you arrive in the heart game. West leads the ◊6 and you win the trick with the ◊A. What now?

It looks as if you will lose just one diamond trick and two further tricks to the major-suit aces. If East has a singleton ace of trumps, however, there is a risk that you may lose a second trump trick. Suppose you lead a trump to the ten or lead a trump honour from your hand. East will win with the bare ace, cash a diamond winner and play a third round of diamonds. Whether you ruff with an honour or with the ♡8, West will score a trump trick for one down.

Although you have no idea which defender holds the ace of trumps, nothing can be lost by leading the first round of trumps from dummy. Cross to the ♣A at trick two and lead the ♡4. East's ace of trumps appears and he plays two more rounds of diamonds. Now you will survive. You can ruff the third round of diamonds with the ♡K, cross to the bare ♡10 and eventually return to your hand with a spade to draw West's remaining trumps.

Finally, here is a deal where you need to find a favourable trump position. Even then, you will go down unless you play trumps correctly.

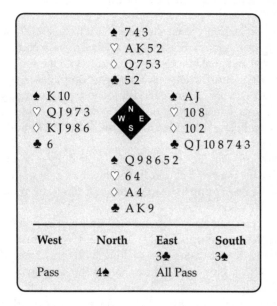

	♠ 743		
	♡ A K 5 2		
	◇ Q 7 5 3		
	♣ 5 2		

♠ K 10		♠ A J
♡ Q J 9 7 3		♡ 10 8
◇ K J 9 8 6		◇ 10 2
♣ 6		♣ Q J 10 8 7 4 3

	♠ Q 9 8 6 5 2		
	♡ 6 4		
	◇ A 4		
	♣ A K 9		

West	North	East	South
		3♣	3♠
Pass	4♠	All Pass	

West leads his singleton club against your game in spades. You win East's ♣10 with the ♣A. What now?

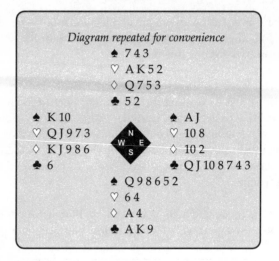

Diagram repeated for convenience

```
              ♠ 7 4 3
              ♡ A K 5 2
              ◇ Q 7 5 3
              ♣ 5 2
♠ K 10                    ♠ A J
♡ Q J 9 7 3      N        ♡ 10 8
◇ K J 9 8 6   W     E     ◇ 10 2
♣ 6              S        ♣ Q J 10 8 7 4 3
              ♠ Q 9 8 6 5 2
              ♡ 6 4
              ◇ A 4
              ♣ A K 9
```

You will almost certainly need the trump suit to break 2-2. Suppose you lead a trump from your hand, though. What will happen then? East will win with the ♠J and give his partner a club ruff with the ♠K. East's ♠A will be the defenders' third trump trick and you cannot escape an eventual diamond loser. (If you are familiar with squeeze play, you may wonder if you can arrange a red-suit squeeze against West. The defenders can prevent this by playing hearts twice, destroying the entries to dummy.)

How should you play the contract? East is the danger hand, the player who can give his partner a club ruff. You must make it more difficult for him to win the first trump by leading the first round from dummy.

At trick two you cross to the ♡A and lead a trump. Suppose East climbs up with the ♠A and returns a club. West will have to ruff with the ♠K! You will lose only two trump tricks, along with one diamond trick, and make the contract. Nor will East fare any better by playing low on the first round of trumps. West will win your queen with the king and cannot damage you with any return. You will play another round of trumps when you regain the lead, again losing just two trumps and one diamond.

Wait to see which discard to make

D ummy has a surplus winner in a suit (A-K-x-x opposite x, for example, or A-x-x-x opposite a void). What discard should you make from your hand? Sometimes you cannot tell without investigating the lie of the other suits and you should delay taking the discard until later in the hand. That is the subject of this Tip.

How would you have tackled this slam deal?

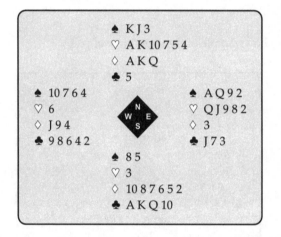

North opens 1♡ and you eventually arrive in 6◊. You win West's uninspired ♡6 lead in the dummy and play two rounds of trumps, East discarding a spade on the second round. What now?

If hearts are breaking 3-3, you could establish the suit with a ruff and return to the ◊Q, scoring an overtrick. Such a break is most unlikely after West has chosen to lead a heart. As we mentioned in another Tip, a spot-card lead in dummy's main suit is very likely to be a singleton.

When the deal arose at the table, declarer drew West's last trump and then had to take a discard on the ♡K. He decided to throw the ♣10 and rely on a good guess in spades later. Since West had indeed led a singleton heart it was most unlikely that he had the ♠A in his hand. Declarer crossed to his hand with a heart ruff and led a spade to the jack,

---

hoping that West held the ♠Q. It was not to be. East scored two spade tricks and the slam went one down.

"You would have made it if you had discarded a spade," observed North. "The jack of clubs falls in three rounds."

South raised his eyes to the ceiling and proceeded to explain that making a spade trick was a 50% prospect – much more likely than the ♣J falling in three rounds.

What did you make of that? The point of the deal is that you should test the club suit before playing the third round of trumps. When the ♣J does fall in three rounds, you cross to dummy with a third round of trumps and discard one of your spades on the ♡K. If the ♣J does not fall, you will discard the ♣10 instead and eventually play a spade to the jack, hoping for some luck there.

Here is another example of the same style of play:

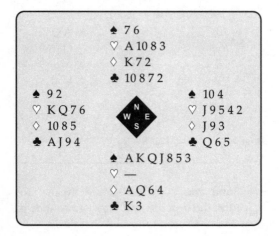

West leads the ♡K against 6♠. How will you play the contract?

Suppose you win the first trick with dummy's ace. What will you discard? If you throw a diamond, you will need to lead towards the ♣K successfully, later in the play. If instead you throw the ♣3, you will need diamonds to break 3-3 (or to find an extremely unlikely squeeze position).

If you were forced into such a situation, you would doubtless discard a diamond. That's because a 3-3 diamond break is less likely than the ♣A being onside. There is no need to make such a guess! You should ruff the heart lead and draw trumps. You can then test the diamond suit by playing three rounds, ending in the dummy. When diamonds break 3-3, as in the diagram, you know that the last diamond in your hand is a winner. You therefore discard the ♣3 on the ♡A, making the slam. What if the diamonds had not broken 3-3? The last diamond in your hand would then be a loser. You would discard it on the ♡A and lead towards the ♣K, hoping that East held the ♣A.

On the next deal you have two discards available and must choose the first one to give you more flexibility later.

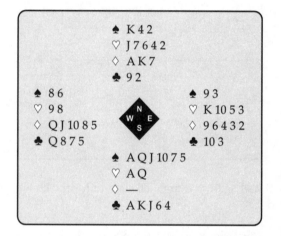

West leads the ◇Q against 7♠. You have two discards available on dummy's diamond honours but cannot tell at this stage whether you will need to throw two clubs or one club. Keeping your options open, you throw the ♣4 on dummy's ◇A.

Next you draw two rounds of trumps with the ace and queen. It's not particularly important but they happen to break 2-2. You cash the ♣A and ♣K, and ruff a club with dummy's ♠K. If the clubs had divided 3-3, or the ♣Q had fallen, you would have used dummy's ◇K to discard the ♡Q. What actually happens is that East shows out on the third round of clubs and the ♣Q is still out. So, you discard your last club on the ◇K and, wishing yourself good luck, finesse the ♡Q. Justice is done, from your point of view, when the finesse wins. The grand slam is yours. If your first discard had been the ♡Q, you would have gone down.

Sometimes you must delay a discard for a different reason. You intend to lead through a defender's ace and your play will vary according to whether

---

or not he rises with the ace. That is the position here:

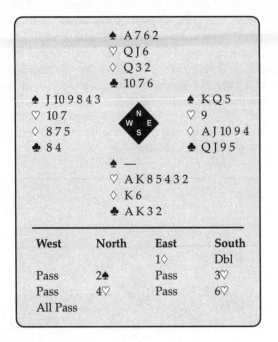

♠ A 7 6 2			
♡ Q J 6			
◊ Q 3 2			
♣ 10 7 6			

West	North	East	South
		1◊	Dbl
Pass	2♠	Pass	3♡
Pass	4♡	Pass	6♡
All Pass			

West leads the ♠J against your small slam in hearts. How will you play the contract?

Let's suppose first that you win the opening lead with dummy's ♠A. What will you throw from the South hand? If you discard the ◊6, East will be able to beat the slam by rising with the ace on the first round of diamonds. If instead you throw a club, East can defeat you by holding up the ◊A on the first round (depriving you of two diamond tricks and a second discard for your club losers).

To make the slam you must play a diamond through East's ace before you have chosen which discard to make on the ♠A. So, you should ruff the spade lead, cross to dummy with the ♡Q and lead a low diamond.

East has no answer to this move. If he rises with the ◊A, you will have two discards for your losing clubs – one on the ♠A and another on the ◊Q. If instead East plays low on the first round of diamonds, your ◊K will win. You can then-re-enter dummy with the ♡J and throw your remaining diamond on the ♠A. You will lose just one trick in clubs because the fourth round of the suit can be ruffed.

Use the Law of Vacant Spaces

Have you heard of the Law of Vacant Spaces? It's a fancy name for an idea that is really quite obvious. One simple expression of the Law is that a defender who is long in one suit is likely to be short in another suit.

Let's look at a particular situation. Suppose that East has two spades and West has six. This means that East has eleven 'vacant spaces' for non-spades whereas East has only seven. If you need to guess which defender might holds a card such as the ♡J, the odds will be 11-to-7 in favour of the defender with the shorter spade holding.

That's enough theorising. Let's look at a deal where declarer can put the Law of Vacant Spaces to good use:

	♠ 8 6	
	♡ A 9 6	
	◇ Q 8 5 4	
	♣ A Q J 2	
♠ A K J 9 7 2		♠ Q 3
♡ 4 3		♡ J 7 5 2
◇ 10 7 6		◇ 3 2
♣ 7 4		♣ K 10 8 6 5
	♠ 10 5 4	
	♡ K Q 10 8	
	◇ A K J 9	
	♣ 9 3	

West	North	East	South
2♠	Dbl	Pass	4♡
All Pass			

West opens with a weak-two bid in spades and you end in 4♡ on a 4-3 fit. How will you play this contract when West cashes two top spades, the ♠Q appearing from East on the second round, and continues with the ♠J?

The ♣K is surely offside, since this card would take West over the limit for a weak-two bid. You therefore need to avoid a trump loser. If West holds the ♡J, the winning line will be to ruff the third spade with dummy's ♡9. East will be unable to overruff and you can then draw trumps (it's unlikely that West will hold ♡J-x-x-x). If instead it is East who holds the ♡J, you would do better to ruff the third spade high, with the ♡A. You could then run the ♡9, picking up the ♡J in East's hand.

So, which defender is more likely to hold the ♡J? As we discussed in the preamble, when West has six spades to East's two the odds are 11-to-7 that East will hold any given non-spade card. East is therefore the favourite to hold the ♡J and you should ruff with dummy's ♡A. When the cards lie as in the diagram, justice will be done. The '11-to-7 on' favourite will romp home and the contract will be made.

The most frequent application of the Law of Vacant Spaces arises when your contract depends on a two-way guess for a missing queen. Let's see a deal on that theme:

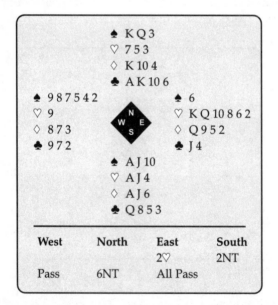

	♠ K Q 3		
	♡ 7 5 3		
	◇ K 10 4		
	♣ A K 10 6		

♠ 9 8 7 5 4 2		♠ 6
♡ 9		♡ K Q 10 8 6 2
◇ 8 7 3		◇ Q 9 5 2
♣ 9 7 2		♣ J 4

	♠ A J 10	
	♡ A J 4	
	◇ A J 6	
	♣ Q 8 5 3	

West	North	East	South
		2♡	2NT
Pass	6NT	All Pass	

You reach 6NT after East has opened with a non-vulnerable weak two-bid. How will you play when West leads the ♡9 and East plays the ♡Q?

It is almost certain that you can make two heart tricks and four club tricks, which will bring your total to eleven. To make the slam, you will then need to guess which defender holds the ◇Q. Who would you say is the favourite at the moment?

In terms of the missing high-card points, the bidding offers no clue. Even at the local church hall they would open a non-vulnerable weak two on ♡K-Q-10-x-x-x and nothing outside. However, the fact that East holds six hearts to West's one makes West a strong favourite to hold the ◇Q. He has twelve vacant spaces in his hand for the missing queen, compared to seven spaces in the East hand.

Fortunately you do not have to take an immediate decision in diamonds. You can perform some detective work in the other suits. You duck East's ♡Q and finesse the ♡J successfully when he returns a heart. When you play the ♣A and the ♣Q, East produces the jack on the second round. A third round of the suit confirms that East began with only two clubs.

Next you cash three rounds of spades. When the cards lie as in the diagram, East will show out on the second round of spades. The odds on who holds the ◇Q have just switched! You have a complete count on the defenders' hands and East started with 1-6-4-2 shape. He is therefore a '4-to-3' favourite to hold the ◇Q. Playing with the odds, you decide to finesse East for the ◇Q. Justice! The diamond finesse wins and you make your slam.

Suppose that East had followed to three rounds of spades instead. His most likely shape would then be 3-6-2-2. Knowing that West held (at least) five of the missing seven diamonds, you would have cashed the ◇A and finessed West for the ◇Q.

Sometimes counting the hand will give you a 100% line in a suit and you can then dispense with the Law of Vacant Spaces. Suppose you have to pick up this club suit:

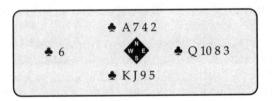

By playing on the other suits, you obtain a complete count on the hand and discover that West holds only one club. You will, of course, cash the ♣A and finesse the ♣9, later returning to dummy to finesse the ♣J.

I n this Tip we will see a little known technique that allows you to duck into the safe hand. When the danger hand follows with the lowest missing spot card you duck, forcing the other defender to overtake.

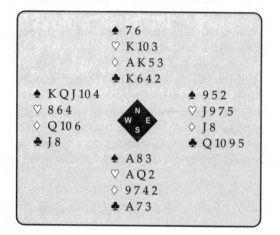

```
              ♠ 7 6
              ♡ K 10 3
              ◇ A K 5 3
              ♣ K 6 4 2
♠ K Q J 10 4              ♠ 9 5 2
♡ 8 6 4          N        ♡ J 9 7 5
◇ Q 10 6      W     E     ◇ J 8
♣ J 8            S        ♣ Q 10 9 5
              ♠ A 8 3
              ♡ A Q 2
              ◇ 9 7 4 2
              ♣ A 7 3
```

How will you play 3NT when West leads the ♠K?

You have eight tricks on top. After holding up the ♠A for two rounds, you must establish an extra trick from one of the minors. In clubs you would need a 3-3 break. Not only that – the defenders could probably arrange that West won the third club (East would unblock the ♣Q if necessary). West could then cash two spades when spades are 5-2.

In diamonds a 3-2 break, which is almost twice as likely as a 3-3 break, will be good enough. Once again, you will need to develop the suit without allowing West (the danger hand) to gain the lead. If you play ace, king and another diamond, you will make the contract only when East has three cards in the suit. A better idea is to lead a low diamond from the South hand. If West produces the ◇6, the lowest spot card out, you will duck in the dummy. East will have to overtake and the contract will be yours. Suppose instead that West inserts the ◇10 on the first round. You return to the South hand and lead another low diamond. West has to play the ◇6 this time or your ◇9 would win the third round.

You duck in dummy and East has to overtake. The game is yours.

Not many declarers would make 3NT on the next deal. Would you?

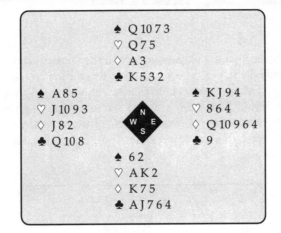

West leads the ♡J against 3NT. You have seven tricks on top and need to set up the club suit. Assuming you have to surrender a trick in clubs to achieve this purpose, how safe is your holding in spades?

If West gains the lead, a low spade switch will put your contract at risk. When the cards lie as in the diagram East can win the first spade with the nine (or jack, if you play the ten from dummy). He can then cross to partner's ♠A for another spade lead through the dummy. One down!

Now suppose that East gains the lead in clubs. However the spade suit lies, there is no way that the defenders can score four spade tricks. East will have to cross to a high honour in the West hand and you can then cover the spade return, leaving dummy with a sure stopper in the suit.

So, West is the 'danger hand' and East is the 'safe hand'. How does this affect your play in the club suit? You should win the heart lead in your hand and lead the ♣4. If West contributes the ♣8, as most of the world's defenders will do, you play low in the dummy! The ♣8 is the lowest spot card out and East will have to overtake unless he is void in the suit. The club suit will then be established, with the spades safe from attack. The contract is yours.

West could have beaten you by playing the ♣10 on the first round. Of course, that is no reason at all for you not to take advantage of his lapse when he plays the ♣8.

Tip

51

**The finesse
you do not
need to take**

Sometimes you hear players saying: "If the finesse is right, you don't need to take it." Do you know what this means? It refers to a deal where a losing finesse would put the contract at risk. Meanwhile, if the finesse would have won you can afford to play high on the first round or two and then concede a trick to the defender holding the missing high card. It's not easy to visualise, you're right, so let's look at a complete deal:

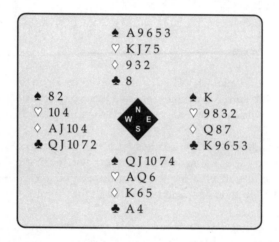

West leads the ♣Q against 4♠. How will you play the contract?

Suppose you win with the ♣A and run the ♠Q. If this loses to the ♠K with East, a diamond switch will put your contract under threat. "If the spade finesse is right, you don't need to take it." At trick two you can afford to play a spade to the ace. When the cards lie as in the diagram, this play will meet with a spectacular success – East's ♠K will fall.

Suppose instead that West started with ♠K-x or ♠K-x-x and you could have picked up the trump suit with a finesse. This hardly matters because you will still make the contract. If both defenders follow with low cards when you play a spade to the ace, you will switch to hearts with the intention of discarding one of your diamond losers. When West has the ♠K, the contract is safe. He is welcome to ruff one of the heart winners with his master trump because he cannot attack diamonds effectively from his side of the table. You may still make the contract even when East started with ♠K-x. You will need him to follow to the first three rounds of hearts, allowing you to discard a diamond on the fourth round before he has had a chance to ruff.

When West started with ♠K-x-x, you will draw trumps before playing for a discard, again making the contract in comfort. Playing a spade to the ace is a form of safety play. You surrender the best chance of making an overtrick in exchange for a much greater chance of making the contract.

Here is another example of the play, this time in a no-trump contract:

West leads the ♠K against 3NT. You duck the first trick and win the spade continuation. What now?

Suppose you cross to dummy with a heart and take a club finesse. You are finessing into the danger hand and will go down if the club finesse loses and West has three more spades to cash. "If the club finesse is right, you don't need to take it." You have seven tricks on top and can afford to concede a trick to the ♣Q when East holds that card. That's because if East has another spade, the suit must be breaking 4-3 and therefore poses no threat.

The advantage of not taking a club finesse – laying down the ♣A and ♣K instead – is that you make the contract when West started with a doubleton or singleton ♣Q.

Tip

52

Do not let the defenders lock you in the dummy

The game of bridge offers you many ways to go down in a contract. When you first play the game, you may go down by forgetting to draw trumps or forgetting that a card has become good. You soon manage to eradicate such flaws, only to find that there are countless other ways to fail in a contract that should have been made.

When you reach the last chapter in a book of Tips for good players, you no doubt expect to see something a little out of the ordinary. You will be the judge as to whether this particular target has been hit. We are going to look at some hands where you can go down by allowing the defenders to lock you in the dummy. You know the feeling? Try this deal, then:

```
                    ♠ A Q
                    ♡ 8 5 3 2
                    ◇ A J 8 6 4 2
                    ♣ 6
    ♠ J 9 7 6 3            N          ♠ 10 8 4
    ♡ K 9 7 4          W       E      ♡ —
    ◇ 3                    S          ◇ K Q 10 9 5
    ♣ Q J 10                          ♣ 9 8 7 4 2
                    ♠ K 5 2
                    ♡ A Q J 10 6
                    ◇ 7
                    ♣ A K 5 3
```

West	North	East	South
	1◇	Pass	1♡
Pass	2♡	Pass	4NT
Pass	5♡	Pass	6♡
All Pass			

West leads the ♣Q against 6♡. How will you play the contract?

Even if you lose a trump trick, you can still bring your total to twelve by ruffing two clubs in dummy. You win the club lead and ruff a club at trick two. When you play a round of trumps, East shows out. How will you continue?

The original declarer rose with the ace of trumps and took the second club ruff that he needed. He then played dummy's last trump to the queen and king. When West exited with a spade, declarer won with dummy's ace and cashed the ♠Q. Needing to reach his hand to draw West's remaining trumps, he continued with ace and another diamond, ruffing with the ♡6. Disaster! West overruffed with the ♡9 and the slam was defeated.

Declarer would do no better to ruff high, of course, since this would promote West's ♡9. Do you see the mistake that declarer made? He should not have allowed West to lock him in the dummy. Before playing a second round of trumps, he should have cashed dummy's two spade winners and the ◊A. When West gained the lead with the trump king, it would then make no difference which suit he returned. Declarer would be able to win (or ruff) in the South hand and draw trumps. This technique – cashing winners in dummy – is known as a Dentist's Coup.

Let's see another example of the technique:

```
                      ♠ Q 8 7 3
                      ♡ A Q
                      ◊ A K 10 5 2
                      ♣ K 3
         ♠ 6                         ♠ J 10 9 4 2
         ♡ K J 10 8 4 2     N        ♡ 9 7 6
         ◊ J 3           W     E     ◊ Q 9 6 4
         ♣ Q 8 7 5          S        ♣ J
                      ♠ A K 5
                      ♡ 5 3
                      ◊ 8 7
                      ♣ A 10 9 6 4 2
```

West	North	East	South
2♡	Dbl	Pass	5♣
Pass	6♣	All Pass	

The bidding is a bit hokey, yes, but there is nothing at all wrong with the final contract. How would you tackle the slam when West leads the ♠6?

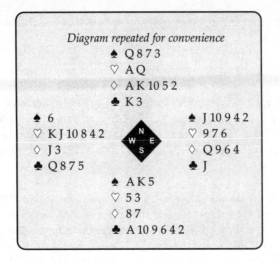

Diagram repeated for convenience

```
                    ♠ Q 8 7 3
                    ♡ A Q
                    ◇ A K 10 5 2
                    ♣ K 3
    ♠ 6                             ♠ J 10 9 4 2
    ♡ K J 10 8 4 2      N          ♡ 9 7 6
    ◇ J 3           W     E        ◇ Q 9 6 4
    ♣ Q 8 7 5           S          ♣ J
                    ♠ A K 5
                    ♡ 5 3
                    ◇ 8 7
                    ♣ A 10 9 6 4 2
```

As always, one of your first tasks it to read the opening lead. West has advertised a six-card heart suit during the auction and has then led a spot card in a different suit. It is natural to suspect that this may be a singleton. The contract will not offer any problems if trumps break 3-2. If they break 4-1, and West's ♣6 lead is indeed a singleton, it is West who is more likely to hold the long trumps. If East has a singleton ♣8, ♣7 or ♣5, you are certain to lose two trump tricks. If he has a singleton queen or jack, you are still in with a chance.

You win the spade lead in your hand and at trick two you must (it's the only way!) finesse the ♡Q. The finesse succeeds, as was a near certainty, and you continue with ♣K. East does produce the ♣J, one of the situations that you visualized. You will now need a Dentist's Coup to prevent West from locking you in the dummy.

If East's ♣J is a singleton, rather than a chosen card from ♣Q-J, you expect West's shape to be 1-6-2-4. You cash the ♡A and dummy's two top diamonds. Only then do you lead a second round of trumps. East does indeed show out. (What heaven! A Dentist's Coup at the table – you will be able to send the deal to your local newspaper.) You win with the trump ace and continue with the ten of trumps. West wins but he has no way to lock you in the dummy. You win the heart or trump return in your hand, draw the remaining trump and triumphantly claim the contract. Such are the moments that draw us to the wonderful game of bridge!